D0983814

THE LOGIC OF
EMPIRICAL THEORIES

MONOGRAPHS IN
MODERN LOGIC SERIES

edited by

G. B. KEENE

THE LOGIC OF EMPIRICAL THEORIES

BY

Marian Przelecki

LONDON

ROUTLEDGE & KEGAN PAUL

NEW YORK: HUMANITIES PRESS

First published 1969
in Great Britain by
Routledge & Kegan Paul Limited
Broadway House, 68–74 Carter Lane
London, E.C.4

SBN 7100 6230 3

Printed in Great Britain
by Willmer Brothers Limited
Birkenhead

CONTENTS

Chapter One

INTRODUCTORY REMARKS

The title of this monograph needs explanation. It certainly sounds too promising. A more adequate, though more cumbersome one, would read: the logical syntax and semantics of the language of empirical theories. An excuse for adopting the original title might be the common positivistic practice of identifying the logic of science with the logical syntax and semantics of scientific language. We are, however, far from claiming that problems of the logical syntax and semantics exhaust all problems in the logic of empirical theories. There certainly are logical problems concerning empirical theories which cannot be classified as questions about their syntax or semantics. The most important of them would seem to be those connected with validation of empirical theories, with the scientific methods of confirmation and refutation, explanation and prediction. The operation of measurement, the role of experiment, the concept of natural law, may serve as further examples of subjects studied within the logic of empirical theories. None of them will be examined in this monograph. The problems which it is devoted to are of a more preliminary nature than those mentioned above. The logical syntax and semantics of the language of empirical

1

theories may be regarded as a necessary prerequisite of any logical analysis of empirical science.

The treatment of this subject in the present monograph needs further qualifications. It focusses on what is characteristic of empirical theories as opposed to others, viz. mathematical ones. Now the difference between these two kinds of theories lies evidently, not in their syntax, but semantics. The formalism of both types of theories is essentially the same. What distinguishes an empirical theory from a mathematical one is the manner in which it is interpreted. This is why our main concern here is going to be with the problem of interpretation of empirical theories, in other words, with their logical semantics. An outline of their logical syntax will be sketched briefly in a short preliminary chapter. We shall not, however, restrict ourselves to semantical problems only. Following the normal practice, we regard the logical theory of language as having three components: syntax, concerned with the linguistic expressions alone, semantics, which deals also with whatever these expressions are speaking about, and pragmatics, which in addition, takes into consideration the speakers—their thoughts, intentions, decisions. Now, in presenting a semantical characteristic of the language of empirical theories, we cannot completely abstract from any pragmatical factors. We could not, without resorting to pragmatical considerations, justify certain semantical assumptions, or even make them sound intuitive and plausible. That is the reason for our frequent pragmatical digressions. The main objective of the present essay remains, however, an account of the semantics of an empirical theory, especially of its interpretation. The fundamental problem here concerns the distinction between the empirical and the *a priori* elements inherent in any such theory. Accordingly, our final task must include an explication of concepts such as: meaning postulate, analytic, synthetic, empirically meaningful sentence, and others related to them.

Any attempt to present in a short and coherent way the main results established in this field of inquiry encounters difficulties which do not arise in other fields of logic such as, for example, the logic of mathematical theories. The situation in the logic of empirical theories seems characteristic of philosophy rather than of logic proper. There are comparatively few results generally agreed upon. There is a notorious divergence of standpoints, proposals, solutions, with regard to nearly all problems within this domain. In consequence, most answers proposed by some authors have seriously been questioned by others. And what seems even more important is a difference in the kind of general approach to the problems in question. Different authors or different 'schools of thought' existing in this field work within different conceptual frameworks, often hardly translatable into one another. In such a situation, if one is to give a simple and consistent presentation of the subject, couched in a uniform conceptual framework, one has to make a choice between different kinds of approach, different languages, different solutions. In consequence, no such exposition can be purely descriptive or wholly impartial. The same applies, of course, to the presentation given in this monograph, which necessarily reflects some of the author's preferences. Let us here mention one of them. It concerns the choice of a particular conceptual framework within which our subject is to be discussed. The one adopted in this monograph coincides with the standard conceptual framework within which the semantics of mathematical theories is presented; namely, the conceptual apparatus of the theory of models of formalized languages. The monograph contains an attempt to apply some concepts, theorems, and methods of model theory (rather simple and elementary ones) to the semantical problems of empirical theories. It follows, in this respect, some other attempts of a similar nature known in the recent literature. (See, e.g. [14] or [18].) This determines to some extent other features of our account of the semantics of empirical theories. One of them consists in restricting the analysis to elementary (first order) theories only. And this is not the only simplification of our exposition. It should be stated clearly that what is presented in the monograph is not a realistic picture, but a simplified and idealized schema of the subject under investigation. The theories considered are much too weak to be identified with actual scientific theories and our treatment of them is based on certain idealized assumptions. A more realistic treatment would be, however, too involved for the purpose of this monograph.

Our account of the semantics of empirical theories has had to be based upon some body of previous logical knowledge, but of a rather elementary character. What is needed here is a first order logical calculus and some elements of the general theory of models. The first is assumed to be familiar to readers of this monograph. In the case of the theory of models, it would be safer not to rely on such assumption. But it is clearly impossible to define within the limits of this monograph the fundamental concepts of this theory in a detailed and precise way; this is a task for a separate monograph. To make the present monograph self-contained, however, we have introduced some of those concepts in an informal and intuitive way; this can easily be done, for their intuitive content is exceedingly simple and clear. All other concepts of model theory needed in our considerations have been explicitly defined in the text.[1]

---

[1]All symbols used are explained as they occur in the text, the only exception being the usual set-theoretic notation. Let us recall it here. Thus, '$x \in A$' stands for 'x is an element of A', '$A \subseteq B$' for 'A is a subset of B'; the union, intersection, and difference of two sets of A and B are denoted by $A \cup B$, $A \cap B$, and $A - B$ respectively; the empty set is symbolized by $\emptyset$, the set containing $x_1, \ldots, x_k$ as its only elements—by $\{x_1, \ldots, x_k\}$, and the ordered k-tuple—by $\langle x_1, \ldots, x_k \rangle$. We adopt the usual abbreviations: '$x \notin A$' for '$\sim (x \in A)$', and '$x \neq y$' for '$\sim (x = y)$'. The use will be made of the quantifiers with restricted range:

'$\forall \alpha(x) (\beta(x))$' abbreviating '$\forall x(\alpha(x) \to \beta(x))$', and
'$\exists \alpha(x) (\beta(x))$' abbreviating '$\exists x(\alpha(x) \wedge \beta(x))$'.

Chapter Two

FORMALISM OF EMPIRICAL THEORIES

From a syntactical point of view there appears, as we have seen, to be no essential difference between an empirical theory and a mathematical one. Either may be characterized syntactically in the same way: as a *formalized axiomatic system*. This characteristic, generally accepted in the case of mathematical theories, is, however, sometimes questioned as applied to empirical ones. We shall take it that the notion of a formalized axiomatic system is already familiar to the reader; it has been discussed in other monographs of this series. We shall, therefore, restrict ourselves to recalling its essential features in a sketchy and informal way. A formalized axiomatic system may be viewed as a result of two kinds of operations performed on a given theory: its formalization and axiomatization. Let us explain them in turn.

I. FORMALIZATION

Formalization of a theory consists in formalizing its *language* and its *logic*. First, the language itself, and then the underlying system of logic are characterized in a syntactical, formal, way, i.e. in a way which refers only to the form of the relevant expressions.

   1. A *formalized language* is usually defined by

enumerating its simple expressions, the primitive signs, and by laying down rules of formation (or construction) which tell us how its compound expressions, first of all sentences, are to be constructed out of the simpler ones. Now, the language L we are going to consider is to be a language of an empirical theory T. How then should it be characterized? We shall adopt here, as already mentioned, an important assumption concerning the type of theories which will be taken into account in present considerations. All of them will belong to the so called *elementary*, or first-order, theories: the first-order predicate calculus (with identity) will be assumed as their only logical basis. This determines the essential features of our formalized language L. It may be roughly characterized as follows.[1]

Its primitive signs comprise three kinds of expressions:

(i) individual variables: $x_1, x_2, \ldots$ (setting $x = x_1$, $y = x_2$, etc., for convenience);

(ii) logical constants: (a) the sentential connectives: $\sim$ (negation), $\wedge$ (conjunction), $\vee$ (disjunction), $\rightarrow$ (implication), $\leftrightarrow$ (equivalence); (b) the quantifiers: $\forall$ (general), $\exists$ (existential); (c) the sign of identity: $=$;

(iii) descriptive constants: $P_1, P_2, \ldots, P_n$ (n k-place predicates).[2]

L is thus, as far as the descriptive constants are

[1] We are not giving an explicit characterization of the metalanguage in which the object-language L is being described, and we are not making use of any device for indicating the use-mention distinction; the context will always make it clear.

[2] We do not mention here the usual auxiliary (punctuation) signs, such as parentheses.

concerned, the simplest of first-order languages, as it contains no individual constants and no functors (operation symbols). But, as is well known, the latter may always be dispensed with in favour of predicates, and so are theoretically, though not practically, superfluous. The notion of a well-formed formula of L may now be defined in a usual, inductive, way. The simplest well-formed formulas are of the form $P_i(x_1, \ldots, x_k)$ or $x_1 = x_2$; all others are constructed from them by means of sentential connectives and quantifiers. The notions of free and bound variable being defined in customary way, we are then able to distinguish, among all well-formed formulas of L, those which contain no free variables, i.e. the *sentences* of L. These are certainly the most important type of expressions, and in our further considerations language L will simply be identified with the set of all its sentences. Let us here call attention to the fact that, so defined, the notion of sentence in L is an effective concept. That is to say, there is an effective procedure for deciding, for an arbitrary expression of L, whether it is a sentence in L. (In nontechnical terms, an effective procedure is a set of instructions that provides a 'mechanical' means by which the answer to any one of a class of questions can be obtained in a finite number of steps.) The effectiveness of such notions as the notion of sentence of a given language is the main objective of its formalization. In nonformalized languages the question whether a given expression does or does not belong to the class of well-formed sentences is often a matter of intuitive, inconclusive considerations.

2. Formalization of language L makes it possible to codify the *system of logic* presupposed by theory T.

Formalism of Empirical Theories

This amounts to a syntactical characterization of the operation of logical consequence in L. The procedure is well known; it consists of selecting a suitable set of logical axioms and laying down a suitable set of rules of transformation (or inference). As both sets are normally infinite, they are specified by formulating, not the axioms and rules themselves, but their general schemata. Then the concept of proof—proof of a formula α from a set of assumption formulas X—is defined along the usual lines, and finally the operation of consequence is characterized as follows: α is a *logical consequence* of X (in symbols $\alpha \in Cn(X)$) if and only if there is a proof of α from X. It should be noticed here that the notion of proof referred to is also an effective concept: there exists an effective procedure for deciding, for an arbitrary finite sequence of formulas, whether it is a proof. On the other hand, there is no such procedure for the notion of consequence: it is, in the case of the first-order predicate calculus with identity, an ineffective concept. Now, with the concept of logical consequence at our disposal, we are able to introduce a number of other important logical notions. We will here mention only two of them: the set of logical theorems of the language L and the set of their negations. The first are called *tautological* or *logically true* sentences of L (*LV* for short); they may be identified with the set of sentences in L which follow from an empty set of assumptions: $LV = Cn(\varnothing)$. Their negations are known under the name of *inconsistent* or *logically false* sentences of L (*LF* for short): $\alpha \in LF \leftrightarrow (\sim \alpha) \in LV$. All these logical concepts admit, as we shall see later, of an equivalent semantical characterization which may be taken as a criterion of their adequacy.

II. AXIOMATIZATION

Axiomatization of a formalized theory provides, as a rule, the only means of its precise characterization. By a theory T we will here always understand the set of all its theorems. So understood, theory T cannot be identified with any set of statements that have actually been formulated and asserted by the scientist. For, clearly, if a certain sentence follows logically from the latter, it will, according to the scientist's intention, belong to theory T as well. A theory then comprises always all of its logical consequences: $Cn(T) \subseteq T$; it is thus what logicians call a *system*. Which of its theorems are explicitly stated and which only implicitly assumed is usually determined by some pragmatical—psychological, sociological—factors, quite accidental from a logical point of view. Being a system, theory T is always an infinite set of statements. How then can it be defined? Two cases should be distinguished here. In the first, there is available an effective procedure enabling anyone to decide in a finite number of predetermined steps whether or not any given sentence in L is a theorem of theory T. In the other case there is no such procedure. The notion of theorem of T is, in the first case, effective, in the second, an ineffective one. A theory for which such a procedure, here called usually a decision procedure, is available is said to be *decidable;* that which does not satisfy this condition —an *undecidable* one. Now any decidable theory can be characterized by specifying the decision procedure, and no undecidable theory admits, of course, of such characterization. One of the main results of logical research in the last decades is that only the most rudimentary theories, e.g. the propositional calculus, are decidable. All others, and among them all actual empirical theories, belong to undecidable systems. For these, axiomatization remains the only means of an adequate and precise characterization. A theory T is said to be *axiomatizable* if all its theorems follow from a decidable subset of them, that is, if there is a decidable set A, called the set of axioms, such that $T = Cn(A)$. If A is not only decidable, but also finite, T is said to be finitely axiomatizable. Now, while undecidable, the actual empirical theories are certainly axiomatizable, for the most part—finitely axiomatizable. They can then be presented as *axiomatic systems*. This amounts to specifying, in some effective way, a set of axioms, A (the operation of consequence, Cn, is assumed to be already defined). If A is finite, the axioms may be explicitly enumerated; if A is infinite, it is usually specified by formulating, instead of the actual axioms, their general schemata. An axiomatizable theory admits normally of an infinite number of different sets of axioms; a particular axiomatization of a given theory constitutes therefore only one of its possible representations.

When treating empirical theories as certain axiomatic systems, we do not claim, of course, that this if just the form they assume in actual scientific practice. In fact only few of these theories have been put into axiomatic form so far (among them the most fundamental physical theories, and certain isolated theories of biology, psychology and economics). What is important for our considerations is the fact that all of them could be axiomatized, if needed, for only as formalized axiomatic systems do they become susceptible of a precise logical analysis. It has been

11

argued sometimes that axiomatization of an empirical theory, though logically possible, is, from a methodological point of view, an inadmissible procedure. It is bound to result in an essential deformation of the given theory. It has been pointed out that, whereas mathematical theories are deductive in nature, empirical theories are inductive theories. And an axiomatic system is said to constitute a proper form of representation for deductive theories only. The objection, however, seems to be based on a misunderstanding. Without attempting an explication of the differences between deductive and inductive theories, we may certainly assume that they depend on the kind of interpretation of the corresponding theories and on the way in which the interpreted theories are validated. Axiomatization of a theory concerns only its formal presentation; it does not presuppose anything with regard to its interpretation and validation. It establishes, loosely speaking, within a set of statements the relations of logical consequence only: it says that one sentence follows from the other; it does not tell us, however, which of them is to serve as supporting evidence for the remaining. A formalized axiomatic system may thus represent a mathematical theory as well as an empirical one, a deductive as well as an inductive one. The difference between these kinds of theories seems to lie, not in their syntax, but in their semantics.

Chapter Three

SEMANTICS OF FORMALIZED LANGUAGES

Our formalized language L, characterized only syntactically, cannot yet be identified with the language of an empirical theory T. It is not really any language at all. Its expressions do not refer to any entities, do not mean anything. To become an interpreted, meaningful language, L has to be given, in addition to syntactical, a semantical characterization. This may be done in a number of different ways. We will here mention one of them for which the concept of model constitutes a fundamental notion.

I. A *model of a* formalized *language* (referred to also as: possible model, semi-model, possible interpretation, possible realization) is, intuitively speaking, any fragment of reality about which this language can speak. In technical terms, a model of our language L, symbolized by $\mathfrak{M}$, may be identified with a $n + 1$–tuple:

$$\mathfrak{M} = \langle U, R_1, \ldots, R_n \rangle,$$

where U is a non-empty set of individuals, and $R_1, \ldots, R_n$ are relations on U (i.e. among the elements of U) having the same number of arguments as the corresponding predicates of L $P_1, \ldots, P_n$, respectively; thus, if P_i is a k–place predicate, R_i will be a k–ary relation. (Unary relations are here identified with subsets of U.) Each model $\mathfrak{M}$ of L may be said to determine one of the possible interpretations of L. It assigns set U to each individual variable as its range, and relations $R_1, \ldots, R_n$ to predicates $P_1, \ldots, P_n$ as their denotations. Set U is called the *universe of model* $\mathfrak{M}$ (in symbols $U(\mathfrak{M})$), and relations $R_1, \ldots, R_n$—the *denotations in* $\mathfrak{M}$ of predicates $P_1, \ldots, P_n$, respectively (in symbols $D_m(P_1), \ldots, D_m(P_n)$). There are, of course, as many models of language L as there are distinct ways of assigning universes to L and then interpreting the predicates of L within those universes.

Given a model $\mathfrak{M}$ of language L we can introduce the main semantical notions relativized to $\mathfrak{M}$. The most important of them is the notion of a formula's being *true* (holding) *in* $\mathfrak{M}$. We cannot here present its full definition, as this is technically involved and requires a number of preliminary explanations. Yet the concept itself is intuitively clear and may easily be explained by means of some examples. We shall apply it here to sentences of L only, trying thus to explain what it means to say that a sentence α is true in a model $\mathfrak{M}$. Intuitively speaking, α is true in $\mathfrak{M}$ if, and only if, things are such as described by α when interpreted by $\mathfrak{M}$. Let α be the following sentence of language L:

$$\forall x[P_1(x) \to \exists y(\sim P_1(y) \land P_2(x,y))].$$

Now, α is true in $\mathfrak{M}$ if, and only if, every object in the universe of $\mathfrak{M}$ which belongs to the set denoted in $\mathfrak{M}$ by P_1 bears the relation denoted in $\mathfrak{M}$ by P_2

14

to some object in the universe of $\mathfrak{M}$ which does not belong to the set denoted in $\mathfrak{M}$ by P_1; symbolically:

$$\forall x \in U(\mathfrak{M})[x \in D_m(P_1) \rightarrow \exists y \in U(\mathfrak{M})$$

$$(y \notin D_m(P_1) \wedge x \, D_m(P_2)y)].$$

If, e.g. the universe of $\mathfrak{M}$ is identical with the set of all human beings, the denotation in $\mathfrak{M}$ of P_1—with the set of all logicians, and the denotation in $\mathfrak{M}$ of P_2—with the relation of one man being wiser than other, then our sentence α will be true in $\mathfrak{M}$ if, and only if, every logician is wiser than some non-logician. The set of all sentences of L true in model $\mathfrak{M}$ will be symbolized by $Ver(\mathfrak{M})$. Sentences of L false in model $\mathfrak{M}$ will be identified with negations of the former and symbolized by $Fls(\mathfrak{M})$:

$$\alpha \in Fls(\mathfrak{M}) \leftrightarrow (\sim \alpha) \in Ver(\mathfrak{M}).^{[1]}$$

Now that we have a concept of 'true in $\mathfrak{M}$' at hand, we are in a position to define a number of other important semantical concepts. In particular, we are able to provide semantical counterparts of such syntactical concepts as 'consequence', 'logically true', 'logically false' and the like, known usually

---

[1] As it is seen from the above example, the definition of *Ver* $(\mathfrak{M})$ determines an interpretation of the logical constants of L. It endows them with their standard, classical, interpretation. We assume two possible values of sentences: truth and falsehood, which may be identified with the universe of $\mathfrak{M}$ and with the empty set, respectively. Sentential connectives may be taken to denote the known functions defined by the corresponding truth-tables. The denotation of the general quantifier may be the unit set containing the universe as its only element, that of the existential quantifier—the set of all non-empty subsets of the universe. The identity sign denotes the relation of identity between the elements of the universe.

under the name of '*L*–concepts'. All of them will here be implicitly relativized to our language *L*. They are as follows:

α is a *consequence* of *X* if, and only if, α is true in all models of *L* in which all sentences of *X* are true:

$$\alpha \in Cn(X) \leftrightarrow \forall \mathfrak{M}(X \subseteq Ver(\mathfrak{M}) \rightarrow \alpha \in Ver(\mathfrak{M})).$$

If α is true in model $\mathfrak{M}$, $\mathfrak{M}$ is said to be a *model of* α. The same applies to a set of sentences *X*. The notions of a model of language *L* and a model of a sentence (set of sentences) of *L* are thus different and must not be confused. We can state now that

α is a consequence of *X* if, and only if, every model of *X* is a model of α.

α is *logically true* if, and only if, α is true in all models of *L*:

$$\alpha \in LV \leftrightarrow \forall \mathfrak{M}(\alpha \in Ver(\mathfrak{M}));$$

α is *logically false* if, and only if, α is false in all models of *L*:

$$\alpha \in LF \leftrightarrow \forall \mathfrak{M}(\alpha \in Fls(\mathfrak{M})).$$

If *M* is a family (i.e. a set) of models of *L*, we shall denote by *VER(M)* the set of sentences of *L* which are true in all models in *M*:

$$\alpha \in VER(M) \leftrightarrow \forall \mathfrak{M} \in M(\alpha \in Ver(\mathfrak{M})),$$

and by *FLS(M)* the set of sentences of *L* false in all models in *M*:

$$\alpha \in FLS(M) \leftrightarrow \forall \mathfrak{M} \in M(\alpha \in Fls(\mathfrak{M})).$$

Let ***M*** be the family of all the models of *L*. We have thus:

$$LV = VER(\mathbf{M}), \; LF = FLS(\mathbf{M}).$$

One of the main results of contemporary logical research, the so called completeness theorem due to Goedel, states that, as far as a first-order logic is concerned, the concept *Cn* defined as above is coextensive with the syntactical concept *Cn* defined earlier (and so are *LV* and *LF*). This may be taken as evidence of the intuitive adequacy of the syntactical *L*–concepts.

II. The concept of truth discussed by us thus far may be called a 'relative' one; it is relativized, namely, to a given model $\mathfrak{M}$ of language *L*, in other words, to a possible interpretation of this formalized language. If *L* is to be an interpreted, meaningful language, we must define, with respect to it, an 'absolute' concept of truth: say what it is to mean for a sentence of *L* to be simply 'true'. This may be realized by choosing from all possible interpretations of *L* the *actual*, or *intended*, one, that is, from all models of *L* (all fragments of reality which *L* can speak about) its *proper*, or *intended*, model (that fragment of reality which *L* does speak about). It is thus assumed that for any meaningful language such a unique model exists. This proper model of *L* will be symbolized by $\mathfrak{M}^*$. Now, with respect to *L*, the 'absolute' concept of truth may be identified just with truth in model $\mathfrak{M}^*$. A sentence α is said to be *true*, if it is true in $\mathfrak{M}^*$; *false*, if it is false in $\mathfrak{M}^*$. Symbolizing the set of true sentences in *L* by *Ver* and the set of false by *Fls*, we have thus:

$$Ver = Ver(\mathfrak{M}^*), \ Fls = Fls(\mathfrak{M}^*).$$

The proper model of *L* plays an analogous role in determining 'absolute' concepts of universe and denotation. The *universe* of L (the universe of discourse) is identified with the universe of model $\mathfrak{M}^*$, $U(\mathfrak{M}^*)$, and *denotations* of predicates $P_1, \ldots, P_n$ (in symbols $D(P_1), \ldots, D(P_n)$)—with denotations in model $\mathfrak{M}^*$: $D_{m*}(P_1), \ldots, D_{m*}(P_n)$. Let us illustrate these concepts using the example discussed above. If the model described there were the proper model of L, the sentence α quoted above would be simply true if, and only if, every logician were wiser than some non-logician. The class of men would constitute the universe of discourse, and the class of logicians and the relation of being wiser than—the denotations of P_1 and P_2, respectively.

This account of the 'absolute' semantical concepts seems quite intuitive in the case of any language whose proper model has actually been determined in a unique way. Languages satisfying this requirement are called *semantically determinate*. But do all actual languages belong to this class? The problem of determining what a given language speaks about is a difficult one; it will be examined later, with regard to language of some empirical theories. Now we can state in advance that with respect to a large class of languages (including all empirical ones) that requirement does not seem to be satisfied. The factors, pragmatical in nature, which decide what a given language actually speaks about do not determine its proper model in a unique way. What is determined by them is not a single model $\mathfrak{M}^*$, but rather a certain family of models, M^*, containing more than one member. If that family fulfils certain conditions —if it is a non-empty proper subset of the set of all models of L: $\varnothing \neq M^* \neq \boldsymbol{M}$, language L may be, and usually is, regarded as an interpreted, meaningful language, though, of course, a *semantically indeterminate* one. Might we then define the 'absolute' semantical concepts with respect to such a language exactly as before? The question has been answered in different ways. There can be distinguished at least three main kinds of its solution.

(A) It has been maintained that we may here proceed similarly as before. We may assume, namely, that there is exactly one proper model $\mathfrak{M}^*$ of language L and define, with regard to all sentences of L, 'true' as 'true in $\mathfrak{M}^*$'. The only difference, in comparison to a semantically determinate language, lies in the fact that the proper model of L is here determined not uniquely, but ambiguously: as some member of family M^*. We define this concept of truth by stipulating that among all models of family M^* there is exactly one model $\mathfrak{M}$ such that

$$Ver = Ver(\mathfrak{M}), \; Fls = Fls(\mathfrak{M}).$$

The ambiguous characterization of the proper model of L brings, however, some consequences which to certain logicians seem hardly acceptable. Let us point out that in language L interpreted by family M^* there may be distinguished three kinds of sentences:

(i) true in all models of M^*—$VER(M^*)$;
(ii) false in all models of M^*—$FLS(M^*)$;
(iii) true in some models of M^* and false in others.

Class (iii) may well be, and in most cases actually is, non-empty. Sentences belonging to it are called *indeterminate*, in contrast to *determinate* sentences from class (i) and (ii). With regard to an indeterminate sentence α, we can never know whether it is true or false: among its intended interpretations are always such as will make it true, and such as will make it false. Yet, according to the definition of truth just proposed, α is ascribed a definite truth-value: it is assumed to be a true or false statement. And this is just what appears objectionable. It has been argued that ascribing to a sentence a definite though intrinsically unknowable truth-value makes an occult quality out of truth. (See [13].) To avoid this consesequence, the concept of truth has been redefined, as far as semantically indeterminate languages are concerned. We will here mention briefly two ways in which this has been done.

(B) Truth and falsehood in L are here defined as follows:

$$Ver = VER(M^*), \; Fls = FLS(M^*).$$

The definitions ascribe a definite truth-value to determinate sentences of L only: those which are true in all models of M^* are assumed to be simply true, those which are false in all models of M^* are simply false. Indeterminate sentences of L are here devoid of any truth-value whatever: they are neither true nor false. Thus the troublesome consequences mentioned above have obviously been avoided, but at a rather high price: abandoning some classical semantic assumptions such as the metalogical Law of Excluded Middle.

(C) The proposal now to be considered consists in replacing an explicit definition of *Ver* and *Fls* by a partial one. The only assumptions concerning these concepts read as follows:

$$VER(M^*) \subseteq Ver, \; FLS(M^*) \subseteq Fls.$$

They qualify all determinate sentences of L in exactly the same manner as all the former definitions. But, in contrast to them, they presuppose nothing as far as the indeterminate sentences of L are concerned. They do not ascribe to them any truth-value, but they do not deny it either. The question is here left open. There are no criteria of application of *Ver* (or *Fls*) for sentences of the kind (iii). This procedure corresponds to a general assumption concerning all semantically indeterminate languages: the concept of truth cannot be defined for them explicitly; it is bound to remain an 'open', partially defined, concept.

Analogous considerations apply to other 'absolute' concepts referring to semantically indeterminate languages. The concept of universe need not be discussed here, for, in the case of all languages to be considered, family M^* providing their interpretation seems to be such that all its members possess a common universe. The concept of denotation has been defined along lines strictly analogous to those pursued in the case of the concept of truth. The following are the main conceptions, formulated, for simplicity's sake, for one-place predicates only. (In formulations for k–place predicates, we shall have everywhere, instead of one individual x, k–tuple of individuals $\langle x_1, \ldots, x_k \rangle$.)

(A) The denotation of P_i is here identified with its denotation in the proper model of L characterized as before; we assume thus that among all models of family M^* there is exactly one model $\mathfrak{M}$ such that

$$Ver = Ver(\mathfrak{M}), \ Fls = Fls(\mathfrak{M}), \ D(P_i) = D_\mathfrak{m}(P_i).$$

(B) The denotation of P_i is here identified with the set of those objects which belong to the denotation of P_i in all models of family M^*:

$$\forall x[x \in D(P_i) \leftrightarrow \forall \mathfrak{M} \in M^* \, (x \in D_\mathfrak{m}(P_i))].$$

(C) We adopt here a partial definition of $D(P_i)$ only; it amounts to including into $D(P_i)$ those objects which belong to the denotation of P_i in all models of M^*, and excluding from $D(P_i)$ those which do not belong to the denotation of P_i in any model of M^*:

$$\forall x[\forall \mathfrak{M} \in M^* (x \in D_m(P_i)) \to x \in D(P_i)],$$

$$\forall x[\forall \mathfrak{M} \in M^* (x \notin D_m(P_i)) \to x \notin D(P_i)].$$

Those two sets of objects form jointly the so called *area of determinateness* (or precision) of the predicate P_i; all the remaining objects belong to its *area of indeterminateness* (or vagueness). Some comments made in connexion with the concept of truth will apply with a suitable modification to the conceptions presented above.

There are, as we have seen, some arguments for and against each of those proposals; none of them, however, seems absolutely conclusive. The problem of defining the 'absolute' concepts of truth and denotation for semantically indeterminate languages remains still open. The conception discussed under (C) appears, as the least restrictive one, the least objectionable. And so, whenever in our further considerations we have to assume some solution to the problem, we shall assume this one. For the most part, however, these considerations will not presuppose any particular solution; they will be quite neutral with regard to any of the considered proposals. Let us note in conclusion that the concept of interpretation determined by a family of models M^*, may be treated as a generalization of the concept of unique interpretation. When M^* turns out to be a set containing only one model, we get a unique interpretation of language *L*. In this case, concepts considered under (A), (B), and (C) become, of course, identical. In what follows, an (intended) interpretation of language *L* will always be thought of as determined by a family of models *M**, referred to as an *intended family of models*; its members will be called *intended models* too.

Chapter Four

INTERPRETATION OF EMPIRICAL THEORIES

Interpreting a theory T amounts to interpreting its language L, and this, as we have seen, consists in determining a family M^* of its intended models. If T is to be an empirical theory, it must be dependent on experience: experience must decide on the truth-value of some, at least, of its theorems. This characteristic of T seems to impose certain restrictions on the kind of its interpretation. We may, in general, distinguish two ways of interpreting a language: a *verbal* and a *non-verbal* one. A verbal interpretation of language L consists in defining its intended models as models of a certain set of sentences of L, i.e. as models in which these sentences are true. This set of sentences will be called the set of *meaning postulates* for L and symbolized by MP. Any other way of interpreting language L will be referred to as a non-verbal interpretation. Now, if T is to be an empirical theory, its language L cannot be interpreted in a verbal way only. Let us consider this point in some detail. Suppose the family M^* of intended models of L be defined as follows:

$$\mathfrak{M} \in M^* \leftrightarrow MP \subseteq Ver(\mathfrak{M}).$$

Let us examine some consequences of such an interpretation. Certain theorems in the theory of models bear immediately on the problem. A theorem due to Goedel states that every consistent set of statements has a model. So, unless the set *MP* of meaning postulates for *L* is an inconsistent one, there exists a model of language *L* in which all sentences of the set *MP* are true. Family *M** is then certainly non-empty. On the other hand, it is not identical with the family *M* of all models of *L*, provided the set *MP* does not consist of mere tautologies. Family *M** may thus be regarded as providing an interpretation of language *L*. But what kind of models will actually belong to family *M** thus defined? Now, *M** will certainly contain more than one model of *L*. The Isomorphism Theorem is decisive here. No set of statements can have only one model. If a model $\mathfrak{M}$ is a model of a given set, then every model $\mathfrak{M}'$ which is *isomorphic* with $\mathfrak{M}$ will be its model as well. Thus the most that can be expected from a set of statements is that any two models of it are isomorphic. A set fulfilling this condition is called *categorical*. Accordingly, if some model $\mathfrak{M}$ of language *L* is a model of the set of its meaning postulates *MP*, any model $\mathfrak{M}'$ which is isomorphic with $\mathfrak{M}$ will be a model of set *MP*, too. Thus every model isomorphic with a model belonging to family *M** will belong to it as well; at best, i.e. in the case of categoricity of set *MP*, all models belonging to *M** turn out to be isomorphic.

Let us realize some consequences which follow from this fact with regard to the problem of interpretation of an empirical theory. We shall, for this purpose, recall briefly the concept of isomorphism between two models of language *L*. Let them be models: $\mathfrak{M} = \langle U, R_1, \ldots, R_n \rangle$ and $\mathfrak{M}' = \langle U', R'_1, \ldots, R'_n \rangle$.

We say that these models are *isomorphic* if there exists a one-one function f which maps U on U' in such a way that

$$\forall x_1, \ldots, x_k \in U[R_i(x_1, \ldots, x_k) \leftrightarrow R'_i(f(x_1), \ldots, f(x_k))],$$

i.e. relation R_i holds between the elements of the universe U if, and only if, relation R'_i holds between the elements of the universe U' corresponding to the former in virtue of mapping f. What this requirement of isomorphism amounts to may be seen easily in the case of a simple language L with one-place predicate P_1 as its only specific term. Let MP be the set of meaning postulates for P_1 and $\mathfrak{M} = \langle U, R_1 \rangle$— a model of this set. Now every model $\mathfrak{M}' = \langle U', R'_1 \rangle$ isomorphic with $\mathfrak{M}$ (and on the assumption that the set MP is categorical—only such model) will likewise be a model of MP. The set of meaning postulates for the predicate P_1 assigns therefore to it, as its denotations in the intended models of L, all sets of objects isomorphic with R. But isomorphism of sets reduces simply to their being *equinumerous*. The denotations of predicate P_1 in models of M^* are thus all sets equinumerous with set R. We may say that the meaning postulates for P_1 determine the set denoted by it only as far as concerns the number of its elements. We do not know at all which objects fall under predicate P_1; we know only, at best, their number. The meaning postulates for P_1 characterize its interpretation in a 'formal' respect only. In the case of languages with other kinds of specific terms, the situation is analogous. Let these terms be, as it has been assumed, k–place predicates denoting k–ary relations. We say that two relations have the same *structure* if, and only if, they are isomorphic. So, in the extreme case, that is in the case of a categorical set of meaning postulates, what turns out to be specified through that set is merely the structure of denotations of the descriptive terms. Such structure of a unary relation (or set) is just its cardinal number. An example of the structure of a binary relation might be, say, a progression. Properties of a relation which constitute its structure possess a 'formal' character. Such structural properties of relations are, for example, symmetry or transitivity. If the set *MP* of meaning postulates for the descriptive terms is a categorical one, all (and only) these structural properties of their denotations may be said to be determined by set *MP*. It is worth noting, however, that, as a rule, set *MP* fails to fulfil even this condition. It is a well-known fact that every set of (elementary) statements which has an infinite model has models that are not isomorphic with each other. A categorical set can therefore be only a set which has exclusively finite models. Such a set of statements must assume the existence of a finite (i.e. not greater than *n*) number of objects belonging to the universe. Its consequences will have to include a 'condition of finiteness' limiting to *n* the number of individuals which statements of the set speak about. A set of meaning postulates for an empirical theory does not seem likely to fulfil this condition. It cannot then be categorical. And as a non-categorical set it is unable to determine even all the structural properties of relations denoted by the descriptive terms: it can determine only some of them. Let us therefore conclude that no set of meaning postulates can apply to a single fragment of reality, i.e. to a single model of a given language, and to no other. No

27

fragment of reality is uniquely determined by the fact that a certain set of meaning postulates applies to it; the same set will apply to any other fragment of reality provided the latter be isomorphic with the former. The ability of a set of meaning postulates to restrict the range of its models is even more limited. Any such set will, as a rule, apply to fragments of reality that are not isomorphic to each other. Consequently, it even fails to determine the relational structure of the fragments of reality to which it applies. The unavoidable multiplicity of possible interpretations of a consistent set of meaning postulates may be well illustrated by the fact that any such set has models whose universe consists of natural numbers and models whose universe consists of expressions belonging to the given language. In consequence, a theory whose language has been interpreted merely by meaning postulates may be thought of as a theory about natural numbers as well as a theory about some of its own expressions!

In the light of these observations it seems obvious that a theory interpreted in that way cannot be identified with any theory in empirical science. Its language cannot be said to be an empirical one. This conclusion can be stated somewhat more explicitly. We may say, namely, that all predicates of language L, which has been interpreted exclusively through meaning postulates, are *completely vague* (except those which in all intended models denote empty relations). We shall explain this characteristic with regard to one-place predicates of L. Let P_i be such a predicate. The question whether P_i applies to an object x is here essentially undecidable—for any object x. As the Isomorphism Theorem obviously shows, among all models of family M^*, there always will be some model of L in which x will belong to the denotation of P_i and some other in which x will not belong to the denotation of P_i:

$$\forall x[\exists \mathfrak{M} \in M^* \, (x \in D_m(P_i)) \, \wedge \, \exists \mathfrak{M} \in M^* \, (x \notin D_m(P_i))].$$

This is true of all one-place predicates of L, with the one exception of those which, in all models of family M^*, denote an empty set. The situation is strictly analogous in the case of any k–place predicate of language L. Now, a language which, besides empty, contains only completely vague predicates cannot be acknowledged to be an empirical one—in whatever way we may define the latter. The question whether an object falls under a predicate must be decidable (viz. decidable on the basis of experience)—at least for some objects and some predicates of an empirical language L. L must thus be interpreted in such a way that some of its non-empty predicates P_i fulfil the following requirement:

$$\exists x[\forall \, \mathfrak{M} \in M^* \, (x \in D_m(P_i)) \, \vee \, \forall \mathfrak{M} \in M^* \, (x \notin D_m(P_i))].$$

Let us then conclude that an empirical language L cannot be interpreted in a verbal way only: its intended models cannot be defined as all models of L in which some sentences of L—its meaning postulates —are true. They have to be determined by some non-verbal means as well. It has often been suggested that what certainly should be determined in that way is the universe of discourse of the given language. It has been assumed that all intended models of language L must have the same universe, and that this universe must be fixed in advance. 'The . . . restriction is motivated by the idea that a formal system is the formalization of the abstract structure of a given set of individuals'. (See [10].) The assumption seems acceptable, as far as the theories to be considered are concerned. We will adopt it here, without analysing the way in which that common universe could be fixed. The assumption, however, is clearly not sufficient to guarantee empirical character to language L so interpreted. To show this, let us assume that the family M^* of intended models of L is now defined as follows:

$$\mathfrak{M} \in M^* \leftrightarrow U(\mathfrak{M}) = \boldsymbol{U} \wedge MP \subseteq Ver(\mathfrak{M}).$$

Thus, every model of L which has the universe $\boldsymbol{U}$ and is a model of the set MP belongs to the family of intended models. It is easily seen that language L thus interpreted still cannot be called an empirical one. To state this in more precise terms, we shall introduce the concept of a *logical relation*. (See e.g. [18].) Let U be a non-empty set, f a one-one function mapping the set U on to itself, and R a k–ary relation on the set U. By R^f we shall denote the relation on U defined by the following condition:

$$R(x_1, \ldots, x_k) \leftrightarrow R^f(f(x_1), \ldots, f(x_k)).$$

Now, R is a *logical relation* on U if, and only if, whenever f is a one-one mapping of U on to itself, then $R = R^f$. A logical relation on a set U is thus identified with a relation which remains the same under all possible mappings of the set U on to itself. The following are examples. The logical unary relations on U (or subsets of U) are: the empty set, and the universal set U. The logical binary relations on U are the following: the empty relation, the universal relation on U, the identity on U, and the non-identity on U. We may state now what follows. Every predicate of L will either denote in all models of M^* a logical relation on U or be completely vague within the universe U. The Isomorphism Theorem is decisive here, as before. Let P_i be a one-place predicate of L that does not denote in all models of M^* a logical relation on U, and let x be an element of U. The Isomorphism Theorem assures that, among all models of family M^* defined as above, there always will be some model of L in which x will be a member of the denotation of P_i, and some other in which x will not be a member of the denotation of P_i:

$$\forall x \in U [\exists \mathfrak{M} \in M^* \, (x \in D_\mathrm{m}(P_i)) \; \wedge$$

$$\wedge \, \exists \mathfrak{M} \in M^* \, (x \notin D_\mathrm{m}(P_i))].$$

Thus, again, the question whether an object x falls under such predicate P_i is essentially undecidable—for any individual x belonging to our universe of discourse U. The same is true of any k–place predicate of L. We must conclude then that interpretation of language L of the kind described above cannot ensure it an empirical character. If L is to be an empirical language, it must contain predicates which are neither logical nor completely vague within its universe of discourse; for some at least among the objects of the universe U, the question whether they fall under such predicate must be essentially decidable. In consequence, the family M^* of intended models of L must, for some non-logical predicate P_i, meet the following requirement: there is in the universe

U an object x which belongs to the denotation of P_i either in all models of M^* or in none of them:

$$\exists\, x \in \boldsymbol{U}[\forall \mathfrak{M} \in M^* \, (x \in D_\mathrm{m}(P_i)) \; \vee$$

$$\vee \; \forall \mathfrak{M} \in M^* \, (x \notin D_\mathrm{m}(P_i))].$$

This is a necessary, though certainly not sufficient, condition for being an empirical language.

In order to meet such requirement, interpretation of L must be given by determining in a non-verbal way not only the universe of discourse, but also denotations of some predicates. The question arises as to what kind of non-verbal interpretation is meant here. If L is to be a language of empirical theory, the question whether an object x falls under a predicate P_i must—at least for some objects and predicates—be decidable on the basis of experience. This seems to determine the character of the non-verbal interpretation of P_i. P_i has to be interpreted *ostensively*, that is, roughly speaking, by pointing out the objects it applies to. Such a procedure, called an *ostensive definition*, seems to be indispensable in order to 'pin down' a predicate to an object given in experience. We shall, accordingly, assume that, among the predicates $P_1, \ldots, P_n$ of language L, there are predicates which have been interpreted ostensively. Moreover, we shall suppose that they have been interpreted in that way only. Ostensive definition is assumed to constitute the only interpretative procedure applied to these predicates. There are no meaning postulates, esp. no proper definitions, for them. They are interpreted in a non-verbal way only. On this assumption, these predicates may be identified with *observational* terms, in certain rigorous sense of this ambiguous expression. The assumption conforms to a widely held view according to which language of an empirical theory must always contain some observation statements, understood in an analogous, rigorous way. One argument in support of this point proceeds briefly as follows. An inferential, or indirect, method of validating a sentence consists in inferring it from other sentences which have already been validated. So, all inferential methods of validation presuppose some non-inferential, or direct, method of validation. It must be possible for the scientist to find out the truth-value of at least some sentences without having first to determine the truth-value of any other sentence. Direct observation presents the basic non-inferential method of validation in empirical science. Observation statements are just sentences which are capable of being validated by direct observation. One can validate such a statement without resorting to any inference—by simply observing the objects this statement is about. Thus the observational statements lie at the foundation of the whole of scientific knowledge; whatever is asserted by the scientist is either expressed in observation statements, or has been validated by being inferred from observation statements. Taking this for granted we have to say that, if L is to be a language of an empirical theory, the question whether a predicate P_i applies to an object x must—for some predicates and objects—be decidable on the basis of direct observation. But then P_i has to be an observational predicate in the sense assumed above. It has to be interpreted ostensively, without any definitional procedures. If P_i were interpreted by means of some meaning postulates, it would be impossible to apply it to an object on the basis of direct observation, without resorting to any other sentence; we should first ascertain whether that application satisfies the conditions formulated in the given meaning postulates, and so to validate some other sentence. The assumption that every empirical theory employs some observational terms of the kind described is by no means indisputable, and, in fact, will be questioned by us later. In this context, however, we shall, for simplicity's sake, accept this assumption without any further discussion. We shall, then, take it that the language L we are examining contains some purely ostensive predicates: $O_1, \ldots, O_l$. We shall call them the *observational*, or simply *O-terms*, and the sublanguage L_o of language L which contains these predicates as its only descriptive terms—the *observational*, or *O-language*. We shall now examine the interpretation of language L_o somewhat more closely.

Chapter Five

INTERPRETATION OF OBSERVATIONAL TERMS

All the descriptive terms of language L_o, i.e. predicates $O_1, \ldots, O_l$, are, according to our assumption, interpreted by means of an ostensive definition. This appears to be a somewhat enigmatic procedure, which is certainly in need of a thorough examination. As we are here concerned mainly with formal aspects of the interpretation of empirical language, we shall not attempt such examination. We shall confine ourselves to some loose remarks which are only intended to make some of our formal postulates more intuitive and plausible. An ostensive definition of a given term is usually thought of as a procedure which determines its denotation, not by describing the object which the term is to denote, but simply by pointing it out. For the procedure to be effective, this object, clearly, must be an *observable* one. But, in a literal sense, we can only observe concrete, physical things. If x is to be perceived by a person, it has to stimulate his sense-organs; so it must be some concrete object. It cannot be an abstract one, such as a set or relation. But this is just what any predicate denotes. Consequently, the denotation of a predicate cannot be observed or pointed out. An ostensive definition of a predicate P_i (let it be a one-place predicate, as before) cannot, therefore, consist in indicating its denotation. When ostensively defining predicate P_i, all we indicate are some concrete objects which are members of its denotation, and, usually, some other concrete objects which do not belong to it. We point out the former as typical instances of P_i (the *positive standards*), and the latter as typical instances of non-P_i (the *negative standards*). Now, the effectiveness of such an interpretative procedure would be evident, were it possible to indicate either all members of P_i or all members of non-P_i. But this is clearly impossible—for all typical kinds of ostensive predicates. If I were to point out all the things which are P_i (or non-P_i), they would have to be not only finite in number, but also accessible to me and to all those to whom my interpretative procedure has been addressed. No ostensive predicate of any importance for empirical theory fulfils this condition. Take the predicate 'red'—a classic example of that kind of term. We define it ostensively by pointing at some red objects and calling them 'red' and, in addition, by pointing at some non-red ones and calling them 'non-red'. But surely we cannot in that way exhaust either the set of all red things, or the set of all non-red ones. And this is hardly our intention. We indicate the chosen objects, not in order to enumerate all instances of the predicate 'red', but in order to exhibit some typical examples of that kind of things, which are to help the person to whom the procedure is addressed to grasp the intended interpretation of the predicate. Such a procedure usually proves successful. Its effectiveness, however, is only of a 'factual', and not of a 'logical' character. An ostensive definition of the predicate

36

'red' may be, as an interpretative operation, 'factually' effective in the sense that it will cause the addressee to understand that predicate just as a predicate denoting the class of red things, and thus will enable him to use that term in the intended way. But that definition does not supply a sufficient reason for such a conclusion. The predicate 'red' interpreted in that way might just as well be understood as a predicate denoting any other class which includes all positive standards and excludes all negative ones. Any such conclusion would be justified as well—or rather as badly—as the 'proper' one. If one chooses the 'right' class as the denotation of the predicate, one is not compelled to this choice by purely logical reasons. This conclusion is arrived at in some process of abstraction whose analysis presents a problem for a psychologist rather than for a logician. Let us conclude then that ostensive definition is an efficacious mental training rather than a cogent logical operation; provided, of course, that it is conceived as above: as a purely ostensive, non-definitional procedure. If in ostensively defining the predicate 'red' we were allowed to make use of some other predicates already interpreted, we could, clearly, determine its denotation in a logically forcible manner. It would be sufficient to postulate that that denotation be a 'colour', i.e. a set of things indistinguishable in this respect from one another. But then our ostensive definition would cease to be a kind of a non-verbal interpretation— in the sense explained before; it would become a true definition. In what follows, we shall take the ostensive definition in its previous meaning: as a non-verbal interpretative procedure—with all its logical problems. What is important for our considerations is that this procedure does, after all, effect an interpretation of certain predicates. We will assume that all O-predicates are interpreted in this way, and we will examine some consequences of this interpretation.

A characteristic feature of any predicate defined ostensively is its *vagueness*. There are always things such that the question whether they belong to the denotation of the predicate is essentially undecidable. The denotation may be identified with a set including those things just as well as with a set which excludes them. If the area of determinateness of an ostensive predicate were simply confined to the class the objects indicated, this characteristic would be evident. But even if this area, as we have assumed, extends beyond the class of standards, it will never cover the whole universe of discourse. Let us here consider two cases: one, of a universe consisting of observable objects only, and the other, of a universe including some unobservable things as well. Some explanation of the concept of observability is needed for the sake of this discussion as the concept is a highly ambiguous one. We shall call an object *observable*, if the possibility of its being observed is guaranteed by some natural law. In other words, x is observable if x has a property P such that the following statement: whoever (in suitable conditions) looks at an object possessing property P will perceive the object—is a statement of a natural law. This loose explication is not meant to serve as a definition of observability. It is only intended to point out some of its characteristic features. As we have seen before, only physical things may be called observable—in any literal sense of this word. According to the present explanation, the converse, however, is not true: not all physical objects are observable. Notice that their position in space and time is of no relevance here. Some things so remote in space or time that nobody has perceived them till now and nobody will do it in the future are observable, while some others are not. Thus a dinosaur is certainly an observable thing, and a gene in its organism an unobservable one. The distinction between observable and unobservable objects co-incides roughly with that between macro- and micro-objects. An observable object is an object big enough, an unobservable one too small, to be seen. This is, of course, a vague distinction. But for our further considerations it is not important where the boundary-line will be drawn. What is important is the indisputable existence of unobservable physical things. They include, among others, such typical scientific objects as elementary particles, atoms, or molecules.

Let us now return to our main problem. If we consider an observational language L_o for its own sake, it seems natural to assume that its universe of discourse, i.e. the common universe of its intended models, consists of observable things only. Let it be the set U_o. It seems clear that even in this case an ostensively defined predicate P_i—for instance, the predicate 'red'—must remain vague. It is, of course, a partial vagueness only. There are elements of U_o which definitely belong to the denotation of P_i, and others which definitely do not belong to it. Every subset of U_o which may be denoted by P_i must include the former and exclude the latter. They jointly form the area of determinateness of predicate P_i. As we have assumed before, this area contains not only the positive and negative standards, but also some other objects, viz. objects which look like any of the given standards. Anything which is similar in appearance to a certain positive standard will be P_i, any object which looks like a negative one will be non-P_i. The trouble is that there always will exist objects such that the question whether they resemble a positive standard or rather a negative one is essentially undecidable. This resemblance in appearance, which is the only criterion of membership in the denotation of P_i, is given by means of a few examples. The qualities in question form a continuous series; we can pass by imperceptible stages from one to the other. So, sooner or later, we are bound to encounter things possessing the given quality in a degree that will not permit any decision. These things may be said to resemble the positive standards just as well as the negative ones. Hence, they may just as well be included in the denotation of P_i as excluded from it. Both decisions will be equally arbitrary. Things such as these belong to the area of indeterminateness of the given predicate. We shall then assume that, for any O–predicate, this area is never empty. The assumption expresses a fundamental feature of any observational language.

This feature becomes still more remarkable in the second of the above mentioned cases. Here, the universe of discourse of language L_o extends beyond the set U_o of the observable things and contains some unobservable objects too. It may be identified, for instance, with the set of all physical objects, U. Such an assumption seems quite plausible, if the observational language L_o is treated as a part of a theoretical language L, which certainly must deal with unobservable physical things. The extension of the universe of discourse from set U_o to set U seems to increase the vagueness of all O–predicates in a considerable way. Let us here advance the following hypothesis on this point. The denotation of any predicate P_i which has been interpreted ostensively, without resorting to other descriptive predicates, remains completely vague in the domain of all unobservable objects, i.e. in the set $U—U_o$. The only criterion of membership in the denotation of P_i is a resemblance in the appearance of the given thing to some of the positive, or negative standards. But an unobservable thing can hardly be said to be similar in appearance to any of the indicated objects. It is impossible not only to perceive, but even to imagine such a thing. All we can imagine is a thing which, surely, must be bigger than the given one and, thus, different from it. There are, in consequence, no criteria of application of predicate P_i to any un-observable object. Any object of this kind may freely be included in the denotation of P_i or excluded from it. Any such object will therefore belong to the area of indeterminateness of predicate P_i. The same is true of all k–place O–predicates. Any k–tuple of objects which contains at least one element of set $U—U_o$ will belong to the area of indeterminateness of the given predicate. The unobservable elements of U form a class of 'indeterminate' objects of a kind different from 'indeterminate' elements of U_o mentioned earlier. The former may be said to 'lie between' the members and the non-members of P_i, the latter, as it were, to 'lie outside'. Their logical status seems, however, the same.

The main issues of the above discussion may be

presented as certain formal assumptions concerning the interpretation of observational language L_o. Models of L_o, i.e. $l + 1$–tuples of the kind:

$$\langle U, R_1, \ldots, R_l \rangle,$$

will be symbolized by $\mathfrak{M}_o$. Let $\boldsymbol{U}_o$ be, as above, the set of all observable objects, and $\boldsymbol{U}$—the set of all physical things. The interpretation of L_o as a pure observational language is given by a family of models M_o. The family M_o is determined in a non-verbal way; predicates $O_1, \ldots, O_l$ are defined ostensively. M_o contains more than one model of L_o; this characteristic reflects the vagueness of O–predicates. All models belonging to M_o have as their common universe set $\boldsymbol{U}_o$. The interpretation of L_o as a sublanguage of the theoretical language L is given by a family of models M_o^*. The family M_o^* is thus taken as providing the intended interpretation of language L_o. It can be defined with the help of a model theoretic concept of extension. We shall here introduce the concept with regard to models of language L_o. Model $\mathfrak{M}_o = \langle U, R_1, \ldots, R_l \rangle$ is an *extension* of model $\mathfrak{M}'_o = \langle U', R'_1, \ldots, R'_l \rangle$ (and $\mathfrak{M}'_o$ is a submodel of $\mathfrak{M}_o$) if, and only if, $U' \subseteq U$ and $\forall x_1, \ldots, x_k \in U' \, [R_i(x_1, \ldots, x_k) \leftrightarrow R'_i(x_1, \ldots, x_k)]$, for any $i = 1, \ldots, l$. We say then that a model $\mathfrak{M}_o$ is an extension of $\mathfrak{M}'_o$ (in symbols $\mathfrak{M}_o \, Ext \, \mathfrak{M}'_o$) if (i) the universe U' of $\mathfrak{M}'_o$ is a subset of the universe U of $\mathfrak{M}_o$; (ii) the relations of $\mathfrak{M}'_o$ are obtained from those of $\mathfrak{M}_o$ by restricting them to U'. Now, family M_o^* may be defined as containing all models of L_o which (i) have as their common universe set $\boldsymbol{U}$; (ii) are extensions of models belonging to family M_o:

$$\mathfrak{M}_o \in M_o^* \leftrightarrow U(\mathfrak{M}_o) = \boldsymbol{U} \wedge \exists \mathfrak{M}'_o \in M_o \, (\mathfrak{M}_o \, Ext \, \mathfrak{M}'_o).$$

As, according to our assumption, set U_o is a proper subset of U, family M_o* will contain more elements than family M_o; and so will always contain more than one model of L_o. It is easily seen that under the interpretation provided by M_o* the denotations of O–predicates remain completely undetermined in the domain $U—U_o$. For every object x from this domain, there are models in M_o* in which x belongs to the denotation of the given one-place predicate, and models in which x does not belong to it. The same applies to any k–place predicate. For every k–tuple of objects which include at least one object from set $U—U_o$, there are models in M_o* of the kinds described above. This characteristic reflects the complete vagueness of O–predicates in the field of all un-observable things.

There are two fundamental features of the interpretation of L_o which are especially important from a logical point of view. These are: (i) non-verbal character of the interpretation, and (ii) its ambiguity. The interpretation of L_o is called non-verbal in the sense previously explained: family M_o* has been determined without stipulating that in its models certain sentences of L_o be true. There are, accordingly, no sentences of L_o whose truth would be guaranteed by the characterization of M_o* alone, with the exception, of course, of all logically true sentences of L_o. These, as we know, are true in all models of L_o, and hence, in all models belonging to family M_o*. Their negations, the logically false sentences of L_o are, in turn, false in all models of L_o, and so, in all models of M_o*. But the truth-value of all remaining sentences of L_o, i.e. all non-tautological and consistent observation statements, is not deter-

43

mined by the characterization of family $M_o{}^*$ alone. Whether they are true or false in models belonging to $M_o{}^*$ depends on what the models are like. Their truth-value might be said to be a matter of experience. These observations suggest certain assumptions concerning the notions of analytic and synthetic sentences of L_o. The *analytic* sentences of a given language are usually identified with its meaning postulates and their logical consequences. As there are no meaning postulates for language L_o, the definition of its analytic sentences, AN_o, amounts to the following statement:

$$AN_o = Cn(\varnothing).$$

But sentences of L_o which follow from the empty set of sentences are nothing but tautologies of L_o; and so, the class of analytic sentences of L_o coincides simply with the class of its tautologies:

$$AN_o = LV_o.$$

The negation of an analytic sentence is called a *contradictory* one. The class of contradictory sentences of L_o, CN_o, will then be identical with the class of inconsistent sentences of L_o:

$$CN_o = LF_o.$$

A sentence which is neither analytic nor contradictory is called a *synthetic* one. In the case of L_o, the class of synthetic sentences, SN_o, will include all non-tautological and consistent sentences of L_o:

$$SN_o = L_o - (LV_o \cup LF_o).$$

All these conclusions seem to be in agreement with what has been said before about the truth-value of

44

sentences of L_o and its dependence on experience. The truth of AN_o and the falsehood of CN_o are known 'a priori', while the truth-value of SN_o may be known only 'a posteriori'—in the sense explained.

The interpretation of L_o, as we have often emphasized, is highly ambiguous. What language L_o speaks about is not determined uniquely. The interpretation of L_o is given, not by a single model of L_o, but by a family M_o^* which contains a number of models of L_o (if their universe U is infinite, their number will be infinite too). This is due to the inescapable vagueness of observational predicates and constitutes a fundamental characteristic of any observational language. In consequence, L_o is a semantically indeterminate language. All that has been said about this type of languages in the preceding chapters applies to L_o as well. In particular, there are the same possibilities of defining for L_o the 'absolute' concept of truth and denotation as have been distinguished before. We shall not recall them now. Let us only call attention to the distinction between determinate and indeterminate sentences of L_o. The class of *determinate* sentences of L_o, DT_o, includes sentences which are either true in all models of M_o^* or false in all of them:

$$DT_o = VER(M_o^*) \cup FLS(M_o^*).$$

A sentence of L_o which is true in some models of M_o^* and false in others will be an *indeterminate* one. The existence of indeterminate sentences is a characteristic feature of any semantically indeterminate language. These sentences seem to be rather useless in any scientific inquiry as they are essentially undecidable. They can be neither validated nor falsified.

To validate a sentence is, loosely speaking, to show it to be true; to falsify it—to show it to be false. But this is just what is impossible with regard to a sentence which under one intended interpretation becomes a true statement, and under another—a false one. Thus the distinction between determinate and indeterminate sentences proves to be quite important for a logical analysis of an empirical language. The observational language L_o is no exception in this respect. Let us note that all analytic and contradictory sentences of L_o will certainly belong to determinate sentences of L_o:

$$AN_o \cup CN_o \subseteq DT_o.$$

This is evident since any analytic sentence is true in all models of M_o^* and any contradictory one is false in all these models. Indeterminate sentences of L_o will include all synthetic sentences which, roughly speaking, refer to some unobservable objects, whereas synthetic sentences, referring to observable objects only, may belong to determinate sentences of L_o.

Chapter Six

INTERPRETATION OF THEORETICAL TERMS

We have assumed that among the predicates of language L there are predicates interpreted in a non-verbal, viz. ostensive, way; these are the O–predicates $O_1, \ldots, O_l$. They do not, however, exhaust the extralogical vocabulary of language L. Being a language of an empirical theory T, L cannot be identified with any observational language like L_o. In addition to observational predicates, L must contain some non-observational ones, i.e. predicates interpreted in a verbal, non-ostensive, way; let them be the predicates $T_1, \ldots, T_m$. They will be called *theoretical*, or simply *T–terms*, and language L, which contains such predicates—a *theoretical language*. We assume then that the extralogical vocabulary of L (predicates $P_1, \ldots, P_n$) may be divided into two parts: the observational vocabulary (O–predicates $O_1, \ldots, O_l$) and the theoretical vocabulary (T–predicates $T_1, \ldots, T_m$). The assumption is based on the fact that any typical theory in empirical science employs terms which obviously cannot be interpreted in an ostensive way. Here, first of all, belong predicates that refer to unobservable objects only: 'electron', 'atom', 'gene', and the like. They clearly cannot be defined by pointing out objects to which they apply.

But some predicates which refer to unobservable objects as well as to observable ones, and even predicates which refer to observable objects only, cannot be defined ostensively either. Take, for instance, predicates like 'magnetic', or 'intelligent'. They do apply to some observable objects, but they ascribe to them some 'unobservable properties', or, in other words, they classify them into such sets as cannot be determined by pointing out some of their members (or non-members).

Now, the question arises in what way, exactly, are the T–predicates to be interpreted. The interpretation of O–predicates which assigns to them their denotations by simply pointing out certain individuals may be said to be a non-verbal and direct interpretation. The interpretation of T–predicates, on the other hand, will have to be classified as a verbal and indirect interpretation. It is determined exclusively by a set of statements which connect the T–predicates with the already interpreted O–predicates. This set is called a set of *meaning postulates*, MP, for T–predicates (or for language L). The elements of MP are sentences of language L which, taken jointly, contain all T–predicates and all, or some, O–predicates. Their being meaning postulates for T–terms consists in the following requirement being imposed on the interpretation of language L: T–terms should be interpreted in such a way that the meaning postulates MP, in which O–terms retain their usual interpretation, be true. The interpretation of language L is assumed to be given by family M^* of models of L. The definition of M^* will thus have to embody the above requirement. This definition may be formulated with the help of a model theoretic concept of prolongation. The concept will here be defined for models of the languages L_o and L. Let us say that language L is a (proper) *extension* of language L_o (and L_o is a (proper) sublanguage of L) as the set of extralogical terms of L_o: $\{O_1, \ldots, O_l\}$ is a (proper) subset of the set of extralogical terms of L: $\{O_1, \ldots, O_l, T_1, \ldots, T_m\}$; and, in consequence, every sentence of L_o is a sentence of L: $L_o \subseteq L$ (but not conversely). Models of L, i.e. $l + m + 1$–tuples ($n + 1$–tuples) of the type:

$$\langle U, R_1, \ldots, R_l, S_1, \ldots, S_m \rangle,$$

will be symbolized by $\mathfrak{M}$. Now, a model $\mathfrak{M} = \langle U, R_1, \ldots, R_l, S_1, \ldots, S_m \rangle$ is called a *prolongation* of a model $\mathfrak{M}'_o = \langle U', R'_1, \ldots, R'_l \rangle$ if, and only if, $U = U'$ and $R_i = R'_i$, for any $i = 1, \ldots, l$. In other words, $\mathfrak{M}$ is a prolongation of $\mathfrak{M}_o$ (in symbols $\mathfrak{M}Prol\mathfrak{M}_o$) if $U(\mathfrak{M}) = U(\mathfrak{M}_o)$ and $D_m(O_i) = D_{mo}(O_i)$, for any $i = 1, \ldots, l$. So, if we prolong a model $\mathfrak{M}_o$ of language L_o to a model $\mathfrak{M}$ of language L, we retain the same universe and the same interpretations of O–predicates as in model $\mathfrak{M}_o$ and interpret T–predicates in any way whatsoever. It is clear that every model $\mathfrak{M}_o$ of L_o has a number of prolongations (an infinite number indeed in the case of an infinite universe of $\mathfrak{M}_o$); but for every model $\mathfrak{M}$ of L there is exactly one model of L_o such that $\mathfrak{M}$ is its prolongation. We shall denote this unique model of L_o by $\mathfrak{M}|_o$:

$$\mathfrak{M}_o = \mathfrak{M}|_o \leftrightarrow \mathfrak{M}Prol\mathfrak{M}_o.$$

$\mathfrak{M}|_o$ is, thus, the *fragment* of model $\mathfrak{M}$ corresponding to language L_o. Returning now to the definition of family M^*, we shall formulate it as follows:

$$\mathfrak{M} \in M^* \leftrightarrow \mathfrak{M}|_o \in M_o^* \land MP \subseteq Ver(\mathfrak{M}),$$

49

or in an equivalent, slightly expanded form:

$$\mathfrak{M} \in M^* \leftrightarrow \exists \mathfrak{M}_o \in M_o{}^* \, (\mathfrak{M}Prol\mathfrak{M}_o) \wedge MP \subseteq Ver(\mathfrak{M}).$$

Notice that in order to belong to family M^*, a model $\mathfrak{M}$ of language L must fulfil two conditions: (i) $\mathfrak{M}$ must be a prolongation of a certain model $\mathfrak{M}_o$ of family $M_o{}^*$; (ii) the meaning postulates MP must be true in $\mathfrak{M}$. Condition (i) guarantees that in any model of M^* O–terms will be interpreted as before: they will retain their former interpretation given by family $M_o{}^*$. Condition (ii), in turn, ensures that T–terms will be interpreted according to postulates MP, i.e. so that these postulates be true. All this seems to be in agreement with what has been said above about the interpretation of a theoretical language L.

The question now arises as to the nature of set MP. What is it like? Can an arbitrary set of sentences of L be chosen for that purpose, or must the set MP fulfil certain special conditions? An answer to the latter question depends on some general assumptions concerning the semantic properties of language L. Is it always an interpreted, i.e. meaningful, language? And, is its being interpreted guaranteed in advance, 'a priori', or is it dependent on experience? There seems to be no decisive answer to these questions. We shall here adopt a view which seems to accord, better than any other, with normal practice in empirical science, namely we shall assume that language L is always an interpreted language, and that this fact is independent of experience. The language of any empirical theory always seems to be treated by the scientist as an interpreted, meaningful language, and not as a mere formal, meaningless calculus. And it seems to be treated so independently of any empirical findings. Experience may decide only whether an empirical theory is true or false, not whether it is meaningful or meaningless. An empirical theory always speaks about some fragment of reality—truly or falsely, as the matter may be. These observations imply important consequences concerning the logical character of the set of meaning postulates *MP*. As we have seen, family M^* may be said to provide an interpretation of language L only if it is non-empty. If M^* did not contain any models of L, L would remain uninterpreted, in spite of the existence of a definition of M^*. We must then assume that $M^* \neq \varnothing$, or in an explicit formulation:

(a) $\exists \mathfrak{M}_o \in M_o^* \ \exists \mathfrak{M}(\mathfrak{M} Prol \mathfrak{M}_o \ \wedge \ MP \subseteq Ver(\mathfrak{M}))$.

Only if condition (a) is fulfilled, L may be considered as an interpreted language. We should, in fact, make a requirement somewhat stronger than the above. We have demanded that the interpretation of L preserve the interpretation of O–predicates given by family M_o^*. Consequently, family M^* must not exclude any models belonging to family M_o^*. If it excluded some of them, it would alter the interpretation of O–predicates by making them more determinate than they were before. That requirement may be expressed by the following formal assumption:

(b) $\forall \mathfrak{M}_o \in M_o^* \ \exists \mathfrak{M}(\mathfrak{M} Prol \mathfrak{M}_o \ \wedge \ MP \subseteq Ver(\mathfrak{M}))$.

It ensures that every interpretation of O–predicates which has been admitted by M_o^* will be admitted by M^*, too. Condition (b) obviously implies condition (a). We shall then require that the meaning postulates *MP* meet condition (b). Moreover, we shall require that the truth of (b) be known *a priori*, independently of any empirical findings. In other words, the truth of (b) must be provable on the basis of the syntactical and semantical definitions and theorems of the metalanguage of L alone. This can be done only if set MP satisfies a rather strict condition which may be called the *semantic condition of non-creativity*:

(c) $\forall \mathfrak{M}_o \, \exists \mathfrak{M} \, (\mathfrak{M}Prol\mathfrak{M}_o \, \wedge \, MP \subseteq Ver(\mathfrak{M}))$.

Otherwise, the truth of (b) and (a) is bound to be a matter of experience. It then clearly depends on what the models of $M_o{}^*$ are like. And, as family $M_o{}^*$ has been determined by non-verbal means, viz. ostensively, only, we cannot be sure in advance that its members will just comply with condition (b) or (a). This can be guaranteed only if all models of L_o satisfy a corresponding condition, that is, if (c) is true.

Let us note here that the semantic condition of non-creativity entails the so called *syntactic condition of non-creativity*, which is usually rendered as follows:

(d) $L_o \cap Cn(MP) \subseteq Cn(\varnothing)$.

It states that the sentences of language L_o which follow from set MP are mere tautologies. Now, every set MP which satisfies (c) satisfies (d) as well. The proof is quite obvious. If the sentences: $L_o \cap Cn(MP)$ were not tautologies, there would be a model of L_o in which they are not true:

$$\exists \mathfrak{M}_o \sim (L_o \cap Cn(MP) \subseteq Ver(\mathfrak{M}_o)).$$

In consequence, there would exist a model of L_o which cannot be prolonged to any model of set MP:

$$\exists \mathfrak{M}_o \sim \exists \mathfrak{M} \, (\mathfrak{M}Prol\mathfrak{M}_o \, \wedge \, MP \subseteq Ver(\mathfrak{M})).$$

And this is nothing else but the negation of (c). It should be noted also that the converse is not true: condition (c) does not follow from condition (d). There are sets *MP* which fulfil (d) but not (c). The proof is rather involved and will not be presented here.[1] Thus, the semantic condition of non-creativity is essentially stronger than the syntactic one, and cannot be replaced by the latter.

A requirement of the semantic non-creativity seems quite natural with regard to any meaning postulate. The most typical example of a meaning postulate for a predicate is its explicit *definition* (equivalence definition). As it is well known, any such definition satisfies the condition of non-creativity, the syntactic as well as the semantic one. The notion of meaning postulate may be thought of as a generalization of the concept of definition. We shall examine the main types of meaning postulates later on. We shall see then what this generalization consists in. Let us now state in advance what follows. Any explicit definition, in addition to the condition of non-creativity, meets a requirement of *translatability*: any such definition enables us, namely, to translate a sentence containing the term defined into a sentence free of it. Now, the transition from definitions to other types of meaning postulates involves abandoning that requirement. Meaning postulates, as a rule, do not satisfy the condition of translatability. But, as our arguments have tried to show, they still must satisfy the condition of non-creativity. This seems to be a characteristic trait of any meaning postulate—whether definitional or not.

We shall then assume that the set *MP* of meaning

[1] I am indebted for it to Mr. C. C. Chang.

postulates for T–terms is always to be a non-creative (in the sense (c)) set of sentences of language L. But which one? How is it determined? In answering this question, we clearly have to resort to some pragmatic factors, in particular, intentions and decisions of scientists who have been constructing a given language and theory. It is their intentions and decisions that ultimately determine the way T–terms are to be understood and, consequently, the set of meaning postulates for them. A set Z of sentences of language L may be regarded as a set of meaning postulates for T–terms only if the users of language L decide to understand T–terms in such a way that the sentences of Z be true—as far, of course, as this proves possible. This does not mean, however, that the whole set Z is to be taken straightforwardly as a set of meaning postulates in the sense adopted by us thus far, i.e. as a set of sentences such that any intended model of language L is defined as a model of all these sentences. As we have just seen, any such set of sentences should fulfil the condition of non-creativity. And so, set Z, characterized as above, may be regarded as a set of meaning postulates for T–terms only if it is a non-creative set of sentences. And if it does not satisfy this condition? Then, accordingly, the whole set Z cannot be identified with the set of meaning postulates MP. It is too strong for that. It appears to contain, besides meaning postulates, some factual statements as well. The set of meaning postulates must thus be essentially weaker than Z. Let us call set Z determined by the decision of the users of language L described above a set of *postulates* for T–terms (or for language L), P for short. We are faced then with a task of isolating the set of meaning postulates *MP* from the whole set of postulates *P*.

How might the set *MP* be determined? On the one hand, it must, as we know, be sufficiently weak to fulfil the semantic condition of non-creativity:

(i) $\forall \mathfrak{M}_o \, \exists \mathfrak{M} \, (\mathfrak{M} Prol \mathfrak{M}_o \wedge MP \subseteq Ver(\mathfrak{M}))$.

On the other hand, however, it must be sufficiently strong to include all of the meaning postulates contained in set *P*: it must be a set of meaning postulates 'corresponding' to set *P*. This is a rather vague notion, which surely can be made precise in more than one way. The explication which will be given here seems adequate enough and, at the same time, possibly non-restrictive.[1] Let us state it in a formal way before commenting on it. The set *MP* of meaning postulates will then be said to 'correspond' to the set of postulates *P* if it fulfils the following condition:

(ii) $\forall \mathfrak{M} \, \{\exists \mathfrak{M}'[\mathfrak{M}' Prol \mathfrak{M}|_o \wedge P \subseteq Ver(\mathfrak{M}')] \to$

$\to [MP \subseteq Ver(\mathfrak{M}) \leftrightarrow P \subseteq Ver(\mathfrak{M})]\}$.

What is the intuitive meaning of the above requirement? It may be presented as a conjunction of two conditions. The first of them reads as follows:

$\forall \mathfrak{M} \, \{\exists \mathfrak{M}'[\mathfrak{M}' Prol \mathfrak{M}|_o \wedge P \subseteq Ver(\mathfrak{M}')] \to$

$\to [P \subseteq Ver(\mathfrak{M}) \to MP \subseteq Ver(\mathfrak{M})]\}$.

This is clearly equivalent to the following simpler formulation:

$\forall \mathfrak{M} \, [P \subseteq Ver(\mathfrak{M}) \to MP \subseteq Ver(\mathfrak{M})]$,

[1] It corresponds to a condition put forward by R. Wojcicki in the article: 'Analytic components of arbitrary definitions' (in Polish), *Studia Logica* 14, 1963.

which states that every model of *P* is a model of *MP*, or, in other words, that the meaning postulates *MP* belong to the logical consequences of the set of postulates *P*: $MP \subseteq Cn(P)$. They are thus obviously meaning postulates 'contained' in set *P*. But do they exhaust all of such meaning postulates? The second of the conditions involved in (ii) states the following:

$$\forall \mathfrak{M} \{ \exists \mathfrak{M}'[\mathfrak{M}'Prol\mathfrak{M}|_o \wedge P \subseteq Ver(\mathfrak{M}')] \rightarrow$$

$$\rightarrow [MP \subseteq Ver(\mathfrak{M}) \rightarrow P \subseteq Ver(\mathfrak{M})]\}.$$

It does not, of course, require that every model of *MP* be a model of *P*; set *MP* would then be logically equivalent to set *P*, and this is impossible if *P* is a creative set of sentences. What it does require is, roughly speaking, that every model of *MP* which 'can be' a model of *P be* a model of *P*. The clause which states that a model $\mathfrak{M}$ 'can be' a model of *P* is here expressed by the following formula:

$$\exists \mathfrak{M}' [\mathfrak{M}'Prol\mathfrak{M}|_o \wedge P \subseteq Ver(\mathfrak{M}')].$$

Literally: a model $\mathfrak{M}$ is a prolongation of such a model $\mathfrak{M}_o$ that in some of its prolongations set *P* is true. Notice that if *P* is non-creative the above condition is fulfilled by any model $\mathfrak{M}$; if *P* is inconsistent it is fulfilled by none. But if *P* is a creative and consistent set of sentences, some models of language *L* satisfy this condition and some others do not. Now, our second component of (ii) demands that every model of *MP* be a model of *P* provided it satisfies the condition just described. A model of *MP* which does not satisfy that condition may be, as far as this component is concerned, quite arbitrary. We might thus say that set *MP* 'corresponds' to set

P in the following intuitive meaning: if only it is possible to interpret *T*–terms in accordance with *P*, then the interpretation determined by *MP* is identical with that determined by *P*.

Let us conclude: a set of meaning postulates *MP* contained in a pragmatically given set of postulates *P* is a set satisfying conditions (i) and (ii). This, of course, is not a definition of set *MP*. First, we have no guarantee that for every set *P* there will be a set of sentences of language *L* satisfying both the conditions. There is no general method of constructing a set *MP* for any given set *P*. There might indeed be no such sets in certain special cases. Then we should have to replace condition (ii) by some weaker one. But, as will be seen later, a set *MP*, characterized by conditions (i) and (ii), can easily be constructed for all typical kinds of set *P*, employed in scientific practice. Second, conditions (i) and (ii) do not determine set *MP* uniquely. If for a given set *P* there exists a set fulfilling these conditions, there will always be some other sets which fulfil them too. First of all, it is easily seen that if a set *X* satisfies conditions (i) and (ii), a set of its logical consequences, $Cn(X)$ satisfies them as well. Moreover, two sets satisfying conditions (i) and (ii) need not be logically equivalent. As we shall see later, there may be, for a given set *P*, sets X_1 and X_2 satisfying the above conditions which are non-equivalent ones, i.e. such that: $Cn(X_1) \neq Cn(X_2)$. The differences between such sets do not, however, seem of much importance as far as the interpretation of languages *L* is concerned. Any set satisfying, for a given set *P*, conditions (i) and (ii) seems suitable for that purpose and so, any such set may be regarded as a set of meaning postulates for *T*-terms. If we choose one of those sets as the 'proper' set of meaning postulates for *T*-terms, our choice must be governed by some additional reasons. It seems to effect the interpretation of *L* in a way which may be of some relevance from a pragmatic point of view. We are going to examine such a situation in detail in the next chapter. For the moment we shall merely consider its general characteristic. The family of models *M**, providing the interpretation of language *L*, might contain, besides models in which the set of postulates *P* 'can be' true, models in which it 'cannot be' true—in the sense explained. In the former, the interpretation of *T*-terms is fixed: it is an interpretation determined by *P*—independently of the choice of a particular set *MP* from all those satisfying conditions (i) and (ii). In the latter, however, the interpretation of *T*-terms may be quite arbitrary: it depends on which particular set *MP* has been chosen from all the admissible ones. And this is precisely the point which may be not neutral with regard to some intentions of the scientist engaged in constructing the given language and theory.

Let us turn now to the problem of further characterizing the set of postulates *P*. It is, as we know, a set determined by a decision of the users of language *L*, viz. by their decision to understand *T*-terms so that the sentences of set *P* be true, as far as this proves possible. But what is the set like? Is there anything general to be said about its content? There is only one characteristic that will be ascribed to *P* in all our further discussions. Set *P* will be assumed to be a subset of set *A* of axioms of theory *T*:

$$P \subseteq A.$$

In consequence, the set of meaning postulates *MP* corresponding to *P* will always be included in the set $Cn(A)$ of logical consequences of $A : MP \subseteq Cn(A)$, i.e. in the set of theorems of theory $T : MP \subseteq T$. The axioms of theory T will thus contain all meaning postulates for T–terms, in particular, all definitions of these terms (if there are any postulates in the form of definitions). This assumption seems natural, provided a theory is always identified with a sufficiently comprehensive set of statements. It is sometimes maintained that some (or even all) theoretical terms of a theory T are defined not within theory T itself but within a different logically prior theory T'. In all such cases, what will be regarded by us as a given theory is not T alone but rather the sum of T and T'. A theory will always be understood to include all theories upon which it is logically based, esp. all theories in which some of its theoretical terms have been defined and interpreted. If so conceived, it surely can be said to contain among its axioms all meaning postulates for its T–terms. Usually we may accept a stronger assumption characterizing the set of postulates P: we may identify it with the whole set of axioms of theory T:

$$P = A.$$

A normal presentation of an empirical theory contains no explicit statements concerning the logical status of any of its axioms. What is more, no such statements can usually be inferred from what we know about the scientist's intention and decisions. So there seems to be no reason for regarding some of the given axioms as postulates and some others as factual hypotheses. All of them seem to be treated in exactly

59

the same way. In situations like these, the meaning of *T*-terms seems to be dependent on the whole set of axioms of theory *T*. These terms are to be understood as denoting those objects which satisfy all the axioms. Theory *T* is then often said to be a theory of just those objects—a theory of 'elementary particles', or 'gravity', or 'utility'.

In all such cases it becomes particularly clear that the set of postulates, here *A*, cannot be identified with the set of meaning postulates in the sense here adopted. *A* evidently is a creative set of sentences of language *L*. Being the axiom set of an empirical theory *T*, it must entail some non-tautological observation statements:

$$L_o \cap Cn(A) \neq Cn(\varnothing).$$

Otherwise, an observational test of theory *T* would be impossible, and *T* could hardly be called an empirical theory. But implying such observational statements, *A* does not fulfil the semantic condition of non-creativity (i). So it cannot be taken to be the set of meaning postulates. Suppose we do treat it this way. Family *M** providing the interpretation of language *L* would then be defined as follows:

$$\mathfrak{M} \in M^* \leftrightarrow \mathfrak{M}|_o \in M_o^* \wedge A \subseteq Ver(\mathfrak{M}).$$

Now it is clear that, so interpreted, theory *T* could not be false. If some of its observational statements turned out to be false, that is, false in all models of family M_o^*, *M** would be empty and language *L* would be devoid of any interpretation whatsoever. In consequence, theory *T* would be either true or meaningless. But it seems that an empirical theory should certainly be meaningful as well as falsifiable.

So, its whole axiom set cannot be taken as a set of meaning postulates. Even when it is treated by the scientist as a set of postulates for T–terms, it still retains its 'hybrid' nature. It assigns a meaning to theoretical terms and, at the same time, it expresses some factual knowledge. It may be said to be composed of a 'definitional' and a 'factual' component. Only the former can be identified with the set of meaning postulates. We have already suggested a way of isolating the 'definitional' component. The set of meaning postulates contained in A may be any set MP which satisfies the conditions corresponding to (i) and (ii) (where $P = A$). So, family M^*, which is to provide interpretation of language L, has to be defined according to our general schema:

$$\mathfrak{M} \in M^* \leftrightarrow \mathfrak{M}|_o \in M_o{}^* \ \wedge \ MP \subseteq Ver(\mathfrak{M}).$$

We have tried to show that this definition ensures for L the desired interpretation. Loosely speaking, it is an interpretation: (a) independent of experience, (b) consistent with the interpretation of L_o, and (c)—as far as possible—with the axiom set A. So interpreted, T is a meaningful and falsifiable theory.

The situation just described, though typical, is certainly not the only possible one. Undoubtedly, there are theories whose axioms, A, can be divided in advance into postulates, say A', and factual hypotheses, A''. Sometimes we find explicit declarations to the effect that certain axioms are to be regarded as definitions and others as hypotheses. In other cases, while we do not find any explicit statements of this kind, we can infer such statements from what we know about behaviour of the scientist, esp. the way he handles different axioms when putting the theory to the test. His behaviour may reveal his intentions and decisions as regards the logical status of particular axioms. Such conclusions, however, are usually far from being unquestionable. Hence—long and inconclusive discussions on the subject. Let us here recall the known controversy between conventionalists and their critics concerning, e.g. the logical status of the laws of Newtonian mechanics. These laws, undoubtedly, perform a double function: they endow such theoretical terms as 'mass' with meaning and, at the same time, convey some empirical knowledge. But which of them fulfil the first task, and which the second? Which of them are postulates, and which factual hypotheses? There does not seem to be available any definite answer to these questions. In other situations, where such answer is available, we take, of course, as the set P of postulates for T–terms, not the whole set of axioms, A, but only the distinguished subset, A'. It should be noticed here again that A' is a set of postulates only, and the set of meaning postulates MP must be determined as before. In some cases, MP will prove identical with A', in others it will not. We are going now to examine in detail the main types of meaning postulates for T–terms and to illustrate thereby these general and abstract considerations.

Chapter Seven

MAIN TYPES OF MEANING POSTULATES FOR THEORETICAL TERMS

In what follows we shall give a brief survey of those kinds of statements of language L which usually function as postulates for T-terms in an empirical theory T. The most important of them seem to be: explicit definitions (or equivalence definitions), conditional definitions (or bilateral reduction sentences), and partial definitions (or reduction sentences). We shall examine each of them in turn, but in a slightly simplified manner so as to avoid some inessential complications. We shall thus assume that language L contains only one theoretical term: one-place predicate T_1. A generalization to a language with m k–place theoretical predicates will be quite obvious. Let us begin with the strictest of all types of postulates: explicit definitions.

I. EXPLICIT DEFINITIONS OF T–TERMS

An *explicit definition* (or simply definition) of one-place predicate T_1 assumes the form of so called equivalence definition:

(1) $$\forall x \, [T_1(x) \leftrightarrow \alpha(x)],$$

where $\alpha(x)$ is a formula with one free variable x, not involving T_1. So, according to our assumption, it is a formula of language L_o, i.e. a formula which contains O–predicates as its only descriptive terms. If the set P of postulates for T_1 entails an explicit definition δ of predicate T_1, i.e. $\delta \in Cn(P)$, T_1 is said to be explicitly definable by means of observational vocabulary. Being so definable, this theoretical term is, in a sense, unnecessary. It can always be avoided in favour of an observational expression, viz. its definiens. As we have seen already, any explicit definition δ of predicate T_1 meets the requirement of *translatability*: For every sentence φ of language L which contains T_1 there exists a sentence ψ of language L_o (which, of course, does not contain T_1) such that the equivalence: $\varphi \leftrightarrow \psi$ is a logical consequence of definition δ, i.e. $(\varphi \leftrightarrow \psi) \in Cn(\{\delta\})$.

Although always replaceable, in the sense explained, by an observational expression, T_1 may be linked with experience in different, more or less direct, ways. This characteristic of T_1 depends on the logical structure of its definiens. Two main cases must be distinguished here: $\alpha(x)$ may be a *molecular* or a *quantified* formula. In the first case, it does not contain any quantifiers at all, or contains them only vacuously, i.e. is logically equivalent to a formula without quantifiers; in the second case, it does contain at least one quantifier non-vacuously. We may now say that all and only definitions with molecular definiens provide finite observational criteria of application for the predicates they define; in the case of a quantified definiens, the application of the defined predicate to a given object cannot be conclusively based on a finite number of observations.

Take, e.g., the following definition of T_1 with a molecular definiens:

(1.1) $\forall x \, [T_1(x) \leftrightarrow O_1(x) \land O_2(x)].$

In order to apply T_1 to an object x we have simply to ascertain by direct observation whether or not x is O_1 and O_2, and this is obviously a finite procedure. If the definition of T_1 assumes a form involving universal quantification:

(1.2) $\forall x \, [T_1(x) \leftrightarrow \forall y \, O_3(x,y)],$

an application of T_1 to an object x calls for a more intricate procedure: we have to decide whether or not the object x bears relation O_3 to every object in our universe of discourse. If the universe is infinite (as, in fact, it usually is), the positive decision involves an infinite procedure; for the negative, one observation may, of course, be sufficient. The converse holds for a definition with purely existential quantification:

(1.3) $\forall x \, [T_1(x) \leftrightarrow \exists y \, O_4(x,y)].$

Here, an application of T_1 needs a finite number of observations, while an application of non-T_1 an infinite one. Both kinds of application of T_1—positive as well as negative—involve an infinite observational procedure in the case of definitions with mixed quantification:

(1.4) $\forall x \, [T_1(x) \leftrightarrow \forall y \, \exists z \, O_5(x,y,z)].$

Now, it seems that all kinds of definitions mentioned above play an important part in actual empirical theories. This, in particular, is true of definitions with quantified definiens. There have been adduced convincing arguments to the effect that the empirical theories cannot dispense with definitions involving quantifiers. A definition of the concept of 'perfect liquid' may serve as a typical example of definitions of kind (1.2): 'A perfect liquid is a liquid which keeps its volume unchanged under *any* pressure'.[1]

There are two points concerning any postulate which are of special importance for our considerations and which are going to be discussed for each type of postulates under investigation. They pertain to the semantic characteristic of the given postulate and thus have an effect on the interpretation of language *L*. The first of them is the problem of *non-creativity* of the given postulate, discussed already in general terms; the second is the question of *uniqueness* of interpretation determined by the given postulate. In the case of explicit definitions, both problems can be answered in a straightforward manner.

1. Every explicit definition δ of predicate T_1 (i.e. every definition of type (1)) fulfils the semantic condition of non-creativity (i):

$$\forall \mathfrak{M}_o \, \exists \mathfrak{M}(\mathfrak{M}Prol\mathfrak{M}_o \, \wedge \, \delta \in Ver(\mathfrak{M})).$$

This well-known fact is considered to be fundamental for all kinds of explicit definitions. It guarantees the existence of an interpretation as determined by any such definition. For any interpretation of *O*–predicates, there is always an interpretation of predicate T_1

---

[1]This definition, of course, has not been couched in observational vocabulary. It would be rather difficult to quote an actual scientific definition satisfying this condition. We will comment on this point later on. In the present considerations we will simply abandon that requirement where it does not seem essential for the argument in question.

which satisfies definition δ. In consequence, any explicit definition of T_1 may be treated as a meaning postulate for this predicate.

2. Does an explicit definition δ determine interpretation of T_1 in a unique way? The answer is: it does, and in a very strong sense indeed. For any given interpretation of O–predicates, there is always only one interpretation of predicate T_1 which satisfies definition δ. The following statement formulates this characteristic feature of any explicit definition δ of predicate T_1:

$$\forall \mathfrak{M}_o \, \forall \mathfrak{M} \, \forall \mathfrak{M}' \, [\mathfrak{M} Prol \mathfrak{M}_o \wedge \mathfrak{M}' Prol \mathfrak{M}_o \wedge$$
$$\wedge \, \delta \in Ver(\mathfrak{M}) \wedge \delta \in Ver(\mathfrak{M}') \rightarrow \mathfrak{M} = \mathfrak{M}'].$$

What is more, the explicit definitions are, in a sense, the only meaning postulates which share the characteristic expressed in the above statement. The known theorem on definability asserts the following: Let P be a set of postulates for predicate T_1. If

$$\forall \mathfrak{M}_o \, \forall \mathfrak{M} \, \forall \mathfrak{M}' \, [\mathfrak{M} Prol \mathfrak{M}_o \wedge \mathfrak{M}' Prol \mathfrak{M}_o \wedge$$
$$\wedge \, P \subseteq Ver(\mathfrak{M}) \wedge P \subseteq Ver(\mathfrak{M}') \rightarrow \mathfrak{M} = \mathfrak{M}'],$$

then there is an explicit definition δ of predicate T_1 such that $\delta \in Cn(P)$. It has been stated only that interpretation of an explicitly defined predicate T_1 is determined uniquely by any interpretation of the O–predicates (and, of course, the range of variables). This does not mean, however, that there will be only one interpretation of T_1 under the intended interpretation of our language L. This would be true only if the intended interpretation of the sublanguage L_o were unique too, i.e. if family M_o^* contained only one model of language L_o. Since, according to our assumptions, it always contains more than one model, the models of language L belonging to family M^* may, and usually do, interpret T_1 in different ways, i.e. as denoting different subsets of the universe U.

We turn now to a type of postulates looser than explicit definitions, but certainly not less important for the scientific practice: the so called conditional definitions.

II. CONDITIONAL DEFINITIONS OF T–TERMS

A *conditional definition* of one-place predicate T_1 is usually rendered as follows:

(2) $\forall x \: [\beta(x) \rightarrow (T_1(x) \leftrightarrow \alpha(x))]$,

where $\alpha(x)$ and $\beta(x)$ represent formulas of language L_o of one free variable x. So conceived, a conditional definition may be regarded as a generalization of explicit definition. (1) is simply a special case of (2). (2) is logically equivalent to (1) provided the condition $\forall x \beta(x)$ is logically true: $\forall x \beta(x) \in LV$. If $\forall x \beta(x)$ is not tautological, (2) is essentially weaker than (1): it is a logical consequence of (1), but not conversely. Only such cases of conditional definitions will be considered in the following. It is quite clear that they do not fulfil the condition of translatability. There are always sentences of L containing T_1 which are not equivalent to any sentences of L_o in virtue of such conditional definition. The class of sentences of L containing T_1 which are *translatable* into sentences of L_o may be characterized as follows. Let δ be a conditional definition of T_1 of type (2), $\varphi(T_1)$ a sentence of L containing T_1, and $\varphi(\beta \land T_1)$ a sentence obtained from $\varphi(T_1)$ by replacing in it each expression

68

of the kind $T_1(x)$ by an expression of the kind $\beta(x) \wedge T_1(x)$. Now, for every $\varphi(T_1)$ there exists a sentence ψ of L_o such that: $(\varphi(T_1) \leftrightarrow \psi) \in Cn(\{\delta\})$ if, and only if, $(\varphi(T_1) \leftrightarrow \varphi(\beta \wedge T_1)) \in Cn(\{\delta\})$. Thus, e.g. $\exists x\, (\beta(x) \wedge T_1(x))$ will be, in virtue of δ, translatable into a sentence of L_o, viz. $\exists x\, (\beta(x) \wedge \alpha(x))$, while $\exists x\, T_1(x)$ will be not.

In consequence, a theoretical predicate T_1 which has been defined only conditionally cannot generally be eliminated in favour of an observational expression. In explicit definitions (1), the equivalence between the defined term T_1 and the defining expression α is not conceived of as subject to any empirical condition which may or may not materialize in any individual case. In conditional definitions (2), the definitional equivalence between T_1 and α holds only for those objects which happen to satisfy condition β. If an object x does not satisfy this condition, conditional definition (2) does not allow us either to infer that x is T_1 or that it is not. Just this feature of conditional definitions makes them a suitable tool for defining some theoretical terms by means of observational vocabulary. These theoretical terms may be said to denote certain unobservable entities which 'reveal' themselves as observable phenomena under certain observable circumstances. Where no such circumstances exist, the entities do not manifest their presence at all. Thus, on the observational level, they acquire the character of dispositions. That is why theoretical terms which denote such entities can, by means of observational vocabulary, be defined only conditionally. Let us illustrate this point of a now-classic example of the term 'magnetic'. It denotes, not a directly observable characteristic, but rather a disposition, on the part of some physical objects, to display specific reactions (such as attracting small iron bodies) under certain specifiable conditions (such as the presence of small iron bodies in the vicinity). The term, thus, seems to be definable by the following conditional definition (oversimplified in matters of physical detail): 'If a small iron object is close to x, then x is magnetic if, and only if, that object moves toward x'. It determines the meaning of 'magnetic' only in reference to objects which meet the condition of being close to some small iron body. If no small iron object is close to x, we can never tell, on the ground of the above definition, whether x is magnetic or not. The definition thus seems to specify the meaning of the term 'magnetic' just to the proper extent. The question whether there are theoretical terms that *cannot be* defined explicitly by means of observational ones has been widely discussed in recent philosophy of science, yet still cannot be regarded as definitely solved. We shall not enter into this controversy. There certainly are theoretical terms which in actual empirical theories *are not* defined explicitly by means of observational vocabulary. Some of them are defined conditionally, and this seems to justify a concern with that kind of potulate. Let us characterize some of their semantic properties.

1. Every conditional definition of predicate T_1 (i.e. every definition of type (2)) fulfils the semantic condition of non-creativity (i). This follows from the fact that any conditional definition (2) is a logical consequence of an explicit definition (1); and, as is readily seen, any logical consequence of some non-creative set of sentences of L must be a non-creative

sentence itself. So, any conditional definition of predicate T_1 may function as a meaning postulate for this term.

2. From what has been said about explicit definitions it follows that no conditional definition determines the interpretation of T_1 in a unique way, unless it is logically equivalent to an explicit one. Unless $\forall x \beta(x)$ is logically true, there always are some models $\mathfrak{M}_o$ in which $\forall x \beta(x)$ is false; and in such cases predicate T_1 defined by (2) may clearly be interpreted in different ways. What is more, all models belonging to family $M_o{}^*$ seem to be just of this kind. Under the intended interpretation of language L_o, β seems to be always a condition which is satisfied by only some objects from the universe $\boldsymbol{U}$. Only some physical things meet the condition of being close to a small iron body. This is just the reason for using a conditional definition, instead of an explicit one. But if so, for any intended interpretation of O–predicates there will be more than one interpretation of T_1 determined by a conditional definition (2). We shall show this for the simplest kind of such a definition, i.e.:

$$\forall x \, [O_1(x) \rightarrow (T_1(x) \leftrightarrow O_2(x))].$$

Let $\mathfrak{M}_o$ be one of the models belonging to family $M_o{}^*$ and let $D_{\mathfrak{m}_o}(O_1) = \boldsymbol{O}_1$ and $D_{\mathfrak{m}_o}(O_2) = \boldsymbol{O}_2$. According to what has been said above, $\boldsymbol{U} - \boldsymbol{O}_1 \neq \varnothing$. Now, in any model $\mathfrak{M}$ which is a prolongation of $\mathfrak{M}_o$ and in which the above definition is true, i.e. which belongs to family M^*, the denotation of T_1 is determined as follows:

$$\boldsymbol{O}_1 \cap \boldsymbol{O}_2 \subseteq D_{\mathfrak{m}}(T_1) \subseteq \boldsymbol{U} - (\boldsymbol{O}_1 - \boldsymbol{O}_2).$$

71

$D_m(T_1)$ would thus be determined uniquely only if $O_1 \cap O_2 = U - (O_1 - O_2)$, that is, only if $U - O_1 = \emptyset$. And this is just contrary to our assumption. So, in different models $\mathfrak{M}$ of the kind just described T_1 will denote different sets of objects, ranging from $O_1 \cap O_2$ to $U - (O_1 - O_2)$. The interpretation of T_1 may be said to be determined only in subset O_1 of the universe U; in the rest of it, $U - O_1$, it remains undetermined. This indeterminateness of interpretation of T_1, called sometimes the 'openness' of its meaning, is regarded as an intrinsic feature of typical theoretical terms. All such terms are, in this respect, like T_1: all are 'open' terms.

Let us turn now to the kind of postulates which might be thought of as generalized conditional definitions. These are the so called partial definitions, or, in a different terminology, reduction sentences.

III. PARTIAL DEFINITIONS OF T–TERMS

A *partial definition* of one-place predicate T_1 is usually formulated as a pair of following statements:

$$\forall x \, [\alpha(x) \to T_1(x)], \ \forall x \, [\beta(x) \to \sim T_1(x)],$$

or simply, as their conjunction:

(3) $\forall x \, [(\alpha(x) \to T_1(x)) \land (\beta(x) \to \sim T_1(x))],$

where, as before, $\alpha(x)$ and $\beta(x)$ represent formulas of L_o with x as the only free variable. A conditional definition (2) might be viewed as a special case of partial definition (3). If in the latter $\alpha(x)$ takes the form of $\beta(x) \land \alpha(x)$, and $\beta(x)$ the form of $\beta(x) \land \sim \alpha(x)$, we get a statement logically equivalent to (2). (Hence

72

(2) has sometimes been called a 'bilateral reduction sentence'.) But (3) clearly comprises such cases as do not fall under schema (2). (3) seems to represent a form of postulates which is very common in actual scientific practice. Because of their semantic properties, however, statements of type (3) cannot generally qualify as meaning postulates for T–predicates.

1. A partial definition, in contrast to conditional, does not generally meet the semantic condition of non-creativity, (i). (3) entails a sentence of language L_o:

(4) $$\forall x \sim (\alpha(x) \wedge \beta(x)),$$

which may well be a non-tautological observation statement. In such case, (3) is obviously creative and cannot be identified with meaning postulate for T_1. If (4) turns out to be logically true, a partial definition (3) becomes logically equivalent to a conditional one, e.g.:

(5) $$\forall x \, [(\alpha(x) \vee \beta(x)) \rightarrow (T_1(x) \leftrightarrow \alpha(x))],$$

and meets the requirements of non-creativity. It may then itself be taken as meaning postulate for T_1. Otherwise, we have to take as such postulate a 'definitional' component of (3), that is, a sentence of L which fulfils conditions (i) and (ii) stated before. Now, on the assumption that (4) is logically true, (3) is logically equivalent to a number of statements, one of which is the conditional definition (5) quoted above. Two others are:

(6) $$\forall x \, [\sim (\alpha(x) \wedge \beta(x)) \rightarrow ((\alpha(x) \vee \beta(x)) \rightarrow$$
$$\rightarrow (T_1(x) \leftrightarrow \alpha(x)))],$$

73

$$(7) \quad \forall x \sim (\alpha(x) \wedge \beta(x)) \to \forall x \, [(\alpha(x) \vee \beta(x)) \to$$

$$\to (T_1(x) \leftrightarrow \alpha(x))].$$

If (4) is not logically true, any of these statements may be regarded as a 'definitional' component of (3) and treated as a meaning postulate for T_1. They all satisfy the non-creativity requirement (i): (5) is a conditional definition and (6) and (7) its logical consequences. And it can easily be proved that they all fulfil condition (ii).

Let us now call attention to the fact that, when (4) is not logically true, the statements (5), (6), and (7) are not logically equivalent to each other. (6) is a logical consequence of (5), but (5) is not a consequence of (6); (7) follows from (6), but not conversely. So (5) is logically stronger than (6) and (6) stronger than (7). It may be shown that (7) is, in fact, the weakest form of meaning postulate contained in (3): it is a consequence of every statement which satisfies conditions (i) and (ii). Thus, we have here a situation described in general terms in the preceding chapter. There are, namely, various meaning postulates which correspond, in the sense explained, to the same postulate, but differ in other respects. The question arises how these differences effect the interpretation of language *L*, viz. the interpretation of its theoretical term T_1. In examining this question, we will restrict ourselves to the simplest case of a partial definition (3), i.e.:

$$(3') \quad \forall x \, [(O_1(x) \to T_1(x)) \wedge (O_2(x) \to \sim T_1(x))],$$

and will present corresponding to it meaning postulates (5), (6), and (7), in slightly modified, more

74

intuitive and conspicuous, though, of course, logically equivalent forms:

$$(5') \qquad \forall x \, [(O_1(x) \to T_1(x)) \, \wedge$$

$$\wedge (O_2(x) \, \wedge \sim O_1(x) \to \, \sim T_1(x))],$$

$$(6') \qquad \forall x \, [(O_1(x) \, \wedge \sim O_2(x) \to T_1(x)) \, \wedge$$

$$\wedge (O_2(x) \, \wedge \sim O_1(x) \to \, \sim T_1(x))],$$

$$(7') \quad \forall x \sim (O_1(x) \, \wedge \, O_2(x)) \to \forall x \, [(O_1(x) \to$$

$$\to T_1(x)) \, \wedge \, (O_2(x) \to \, \sim T_1(x))].$$

Let $\mathfrak{M}_o$ be a model of family $M_o{}^*$, and let $D_{mo}(O_1) = \boldsymbol{O}_1$ and $D_{mo}(O_2) = \boldsymbol{O}_2$. We shall distinguish two cases, according to whether the statement:

$$(4') \qquad \forall x \sim (O_1(x) \, \wedge \, O_2(x))$$

is true in $\mathfrak{M}_o$ or not, i.e. whether $\boldsymbol{O}_1 \cap \boldsymbol{O}_2 = \varnothing$ or not. In the first case, any model of language L which is a prolongation of $\mathfrak{M}_o$ 'can be' a model of definition $(3')$, and so all the postulates $(5')$, $(6')$, and $(7')$, according to condition (ii), determine the interpretation of T_1 in exactly the same way: in accordance with definition $(3')$. The denotation of T_1 is here defined as follows:

$$\boldsymbol{O}_1 \subseteq D_m(T_1) \subseteq \boldsymbol{U} - \boldsymbol{O}_2.$$

It is thus determined for all elements of the set $\boldsymbol{O}_1 \cup \boldsymbol{O}_2$ (it is, in this set, identical with $\boldsymbol{O}_1$) and undetermined for all other objects from the universe $\boldsymbol{U} : \boldsymbol{U} - (\boldsymbol{O}_1 \cup \boldsymbol{O}_2)$. In the second case, no model of language L which is a prolongation of $\mathfrak{M}_o$ 'can be' a model of definition $(3')$. In these models, i.e. in models in which $\boldsymbol{O}_1 \cap \boldsymbol{O}_2 \neq \varnothing$, different postulates —$(5')$, $(6')$, $(7')$—determine different interpretations

75

of T_1. According to (5'), the interpretation of T_1 is, as before, undetermined only for elements of the set $U - (O_1 \cup O_2)$; for objects from the set $O_1 \cup O_2$ it is determined and identical with O_1. But as now the latter include elements of $O_1 \cap O_2$, these will also belong to the denotation of T_1, in contrast to the former case. According to (6'), the interpretation of T_1 is undetermined not only for elements of the set $U - (O_1 \cup O_2)$ but also for elements of $O_1 \cap O_2$; for the remaining objects from U it is determined and identical with $O_1 - O_2$. According to (7'), the interpretation of T_1 is, in the case under consideration, completely undetermined: $D_m(T_1)$ may be any subset of U whatsoever. All these differences in interpretation of T_1 might seem, in a sense, inessential. If in models of $M_o{}^*$ sentence (4') turns out to be false, the partial definition (3') will be false too (or, at least, indeterminate, provided (4') is false in some only models of $M_o{}^*$). It should then be rejected, or altered so as not to imply such consequences. It must be admitted, however, that there might be some additional reasons for preferring one of the above possibilities. The intentions of the scientist seem here decisive.

2. As the preceding analysis has clearly shown, the interpretation of predicate T_1, as introduced by a partial definition (3), could be determined uniquely by a model $\mathfrak{M}_o$ of language L_o only if the sentence $\forall x(\alpha(x) \lor \beta(x))$ were true in $\mathfrak{M}_o$. But, in fact, models of family $M_o{}^*$ hardly satisfy this condition. A partial definition is really needed only when the condition is not satisfied. Otherwise, we could manage with explicit definitions alone.

Main Types of Meaning Postulates

A few words still need to be added about some other kinds of postulates which, on a closer scrutiny, turn out to be reducible to the ones already considered. It has sometimes been maintained that the meaning postulate for a predicate T_1 may be identical with one only of the statements constituting a partial definition. It may state criteria of application either for T_1 or for non-T_1 only. Such 'unilateral reduction sentences', as they are sometimes called, are clearly equivalent to certain 'degenerate' cases of conditional definition. $\forall x[\alpha(x) \to T_1(x)]$ is logically equivalent to $\forall x[\alpha(x) \to (T_1(x) \leftrightarrow \alpha(x))]$, and $\forall x[\beta(x) \to \sim T_1(x)]$ to $\forall x[\beta(x) \to (T_1(x) \leftrightarrow \sim \beta(x))]$. On the other hand, the postulate for a predicate T_1 may consist of two and more conditional definitions. This kind of postulate undoubtedly plays an important role in defining theoretical terms in actual empirical theories. Every term defined only conditionally remains, as we have seen, partly undetermined. This indeterminacy may be, and usually is, decreased by laying down additional conditional definitions which refer to different criteria of application. Thus, e.g. the conditional definition of predicate 'magnetic' quoted above might be supplemented by the following one: 'If x moves through a closed wire loop, then x is magnetic if and only if an electric current flows in the loop'. The definitions together provide criteria of application for the term 'magnetic' with reference to any object that satisfies the condition of at least one of them. Now, these two conditional definitions for predicate T_1 amount jointly to a partial definition of type (3). Let them read as follows:

$$\forall x[\beta(x) \to (T_1(x) \leftrightarrow \alpha(x))],$$
$$\forall x[\delta(x) \to (T_1(x) \leftrightarrow \gamma(x))].$$

77

Their conjunction is logically equivalent to a partial definition:

$$\forall x\{[(\beta(x) \wedge \alpha(x) \vee \delta(x) \wedge \gamma(x)) \to T_1(x)] \wedge$$
$$\wedge \ [(\beta(x) \wedge \sim \alpha(x) \vee \delta(x) \wedge \sim \gamma(x)) \to \sim T_1(x)]\}.$$

Thus, all that has been said about partial definitions in general applies to this particular case. One point here calls for special attention: in contrast to one conditional definition, a set of two (or more) such definitions for one theoretical term is, as a rule, a creative set of postulates.

Chapter Eight

SOME OTHER KINDS OF MEANING POSTULATES FOR THEORETICAL TERMS

The types of postulates examined in the preceding chapter do not exhaust all kinds of statements which function as meaning postulates in existing empirical theories. Space does not permit a comprehensive treatment of all the remaining kinds. (Indeed the problems that arise in this connection are far from being solved as yet.) So, we are going to present only some of them: first of all, those which have been suggested by recent writings on the subject. (See [16].) We shall characterize them in outline only and by means of schematic examples rather than in general terms. As previously, we shall, for the most part, confine our analysis to one-place theoretical predicates, but without restricting ourselves to one predicate only.

One kind of statement functioning as a meaning postulate, not so far considered, can be regarded as a generalization, in turn, of reduction sentences (partial definitions) for T–terms and called generalized reduction sentences.

I. GENERALIZED REDUCTION SENTENCES FOR T–TERMS

This kind of postulate differs from all those we have so far considered in one important respect. All

Some Other Kinds of Meaning Postulates

previous postulates provided observational criteria of application for single theoretical terms, e.g. for T_1. In contrast to this, a generalized reduction sentence provides such criteria for a truth-function of a number of theoretical terms, and not for the single ones. It is, in a sense, a much looser kind of postulate than any of the former. We shall illustrate it by the simplest case of generalized reduction sentences for two theoretical terms: one-place predicates T_1 and T_2. A *generalized reduction sentence* for T_1 and T_2 may be identified with any of the following statements or a conjunction of any number of them:

(1.1) $\forall x[\alpha(x) \to (T_1(x) \lor T_2(x))]$,

(1.2) $\forall x[\beta(x) \to (T_1(x) \lor \sim T_2(x))]$,

(1.3) $\forall x[\gamma(x) \to (\sim T_1(x) \lor T_2(x))]$,

(1.4) $\forall x[\delta(x) \to (\sim T_1(x) \lor \sim T_2(x))]$.

Here, as before, the antecedents $\alpha(x), \beta(x), \gamma(x)$, and $\delta(x)$ are formulas of L_o of one free variable x. Let us notice that by means of statements of the types (1.1)–(1.4) it is possible to formulate observational criteria of application for any truth-function of T_1 and T_2 whatever, since any such truth-function can be expressed in conjunctive normal form as a conjunction of some of the disjunctions contained in (1.1)–(1.4). Thus, e.g. criteria of application for an equivalence of T_1 and T_2:

$$\forall x[\alpha(x) \to (T_1(x) \leftrightarrow T_2(x))]$$

may be formulated as a conjunction of two statements of kind (1.2) and (1.3):

$$\forall x[\alpha(x) \to (T_1(x) \lor \sim T_2(x))],$$
$$\forall x[\alpha(x) \to (\sim T_1(x) \lor T_2(x))].$$

Some Other Kinds of Meaning Postulates

It should also be noticed that conjunctions of certain statements from the list (1.1)–(1.4) provide observational criteria of application for the single terms T_1 or T_2: they entail, that is, one of the proper reduction sentences for T_1 or T_2. Thus, a conjunction (1.1) $\wedge$ (1.2) yields criteria of application for T_1, (1.3) $\wedge$ (1.4) for non-T_1, (1.1) $\wedge$ (1.3) for T_2, (1.2) $\wedge$ (1.4) for non-T_2. But conjunctions of certain other statements from the list and, especially, all single statements (1.1), (1.2), (1.3), and (1.4) do not provide any criteria of that kind. Take, e.g. a generalized reduction sentence of type (1.1). It does not formulate any observational criteria of application for T_1 (or T_2) taken separately. What it does state may be rendered as follows: Any object which has an observable property α must be T_1, unless it is T_2.

The question might arise what is the use, if any, of theoretical predicates, like T_1, in actual scientific practice. Now, it has been argued that theoretical terms introduced by meaning postulates of the kind just described play a significant part in empirical science. According to all preceding types of meaning postulates, some observational results are absolutely conclusive evidence for certain sentences applying T–terms. In virtue of a proper reduction sentence for T_1, e.g. any object which turns out to be α must certainly be T_1. Yet this does not seem in accordance with scientific practice concerning an important class of theoretical terms. For those terms no observational findings seem to constitute absolutely reliable criteria of application. All purely observational criteria should here be taken with the tacit understanding 'unless there are disturbing factors'. The description of these criteria must admit of exceptions in case of any disturbing factors, and the inclusion of such escape clauses cannot be carried out within a purely observational language. It seems thus that postulates which are to introduce the terms in question will have to assume the form of certain generalized reduction sentences. What a statement of type (1.1) amounts to is, as we have seen, a postulate for, say, T_1 of the kind just required. It allows us to apply predicate T_1 to an object x which bears an observable characteristic α only under the condition that x is not in a theoretical state T_2. The term 'magnetic', considered by us previously, appears, on a closer scrutiny, to be just of this kind. A postulate for it, when formulated strictly, should assume the form of a generalized reduction sentence rather than a conditional definition.

Some semantic properties of generalized reduction sentences deserve attention:

1. All generalized reduction sentences corresponding to (1.1)–(1.4), that is, all the statements (1.1)–(1.4) and all their conjunctions, fulfil the semantic condition of non-creativity (i)—except the conjunction of all the statements listed: (1.1) $\land$ (1.2) $\land$ (1.3) $\land$ (1.4). This conjunction entails the following sentence of language L_o:

(1.5) $\forall x \sim (\alpha(x) \land \beta(x) \land \gamma(x) \land \delta(x))$.

Unless (1.5) is logically true, the conjunction is a creative sentence of language L. We must then take some weaker sentence of L, fulfilling conditions (i) and (ii), as the meaning postulate contained in this conjunction, e.g. the following one:

$$(1.5) \rightarrow (1.1) \land (1.2) \land (1.3) \land (1.4).$$

2. The admission of generalized reduction sentences

as meaning postulates for T-terms means a considerable liberalization of the concept of interpretation. Some of the generalized reduction sentences determine the interpretation of the given T-terms not only ambiguously, but to a very slight extent indeed. A statement of kind (1.1), e.g. imposes a restriction only on the joint interpretation of terms T_1 and T_2, and, in addition, it does not determine it uniquely, for any intended interpretation of O-predicates. Interpretations of the single terms remain completely undetermined. T_1, e.g. may denote any subset of the universe U, unless it is governed by some other meaning postulates besides (1.1). It is thus, in a sense, completely vague. Hence the empirical meaningfulness of such terms has sometimes been questioned. We cannot enter into this discussion in the present context.

The statements (1.1)–(1.4) present the simplest case of generalized reduction sentences. Statements yielding generalized reduction sentences in their most general form might be characterized by bringing out the main differences between them and the simple statements quoted above. The differences could, roughly, be stated as follows:

(1) the observational antecedents may be any formulas of L_o whatsoever;

(2) the consequents may contain m k-place T-predicates;

(3) any k-place $(k > 1)$ T-predicate may appear with different variables in place of its different arguments;

(4) any T-predicate may appear more than once in a given statement.

83

We might also count as generalized reduction sentences certain 'degenerate' cases of statements just characterized: sentences without any observational antecedent and sentences without any theoretical consequent altogether. If the concept of a generalized reduction sentence is understood in such a broad manner, all other kinds of meaning postulates for T-predicates in language L will fall into a class of statements which may be called *meaning postulates with T-terms 'controlled' by an existential quantifier.* A theorem due to Stopes-Roe states that all sentences of L which are not logically equivalent to generalized reduction sentences ('degenerate' cases included) contain T-terms 'controlled' by an existential quantifier.

II. Meaning Postulates with T-Terms 'Controlled' by an Existential Quantifier

A general characteristic of this class of statements is too involved to be given here. Besides, the class clearly comprises many kinds of statements which do not seem likely to occur as meaning postulates for theoretical terms in any actual empirical theory. We shall thus restrict ourselves to some schematic examples and a few general comments. The most important kind of the statements under consideration seems to consist of sentences which might be characterized as follows: when the sentence is reduced to prenex normal form, it contains at least once occurrence of a T-predicate such that an argument of it is bound by an existential quantifier. The simplest cases of such statements are:

(2.1) $\forall x[\alpha(x) \rightarrow \exists y\ T_1(y)]$,

or

(2.2) $\forall x[\alpha(x) \rightarrow \exists y\ T_2(x,y)]$,

but they do not seem to represent any useful meaning postulates. A type which appears more suitable for that purpose may be rendered as follows:

(2.3) $\forall x[\alpha(x) \rightarrow \exists y\ (T_2(y,x) \wedge T_1(y))]$.

Here, as usual, $\alpha(x)$ is a formula of L_o with x as its only free variable. It seems that a statement of type (2.3) can really function as a meaning postulate for T_1 provided T_2 has already been interpreted by means of other meaning postulates besides (2.3).

What kind of theoretical terms can a predicate, like T_1, stand for? Let us here recall a distinction made between two kinds of theoretical terms. One of them contains predicates which refer to unobservable objects only; the other those which also (or exclusively) refer to some observable things. Predicates of the first kind (theoretical terms in the strict meaning) may be exemplified by predicates, like 'electron', 'atom', 'gene'. Now, statement (2.3) seems to be suitable for introducing just those kinds of theoretical terms. Notice that they cannot be introduced by a reduction sentence of the type:

$$\forall x[\alpha(x) \rightarrow T_1(x)],$$

nor by any similar generalized reduction sentence. As T_1 is to refer to unobservable objects only, α cannot refer to any observable ones. Yet α, as an expression of language L_o, contains as its descriptive terms exclusively O–predicates, which, it has been assumed, are completely undetermined in the set of all unobservable objects, $U - U_o$. In effect, α does not, in a sense, refer to any unobservable objects either: it may be shown that under some intended interpretation of language L_o, i.e. in some model of family $M_o{}^*$, no object from the set $U - U_o$ satisfies the condition α. It seems thus quite intuitive (and so we omit here any formal proof) that in such a case the above reduction sentence fails to put any intrinsic restriction on the interpretation of T_1. So, it cannot function as a meaning postulate for this kind of term. As such a postulate can, of course, serve a reduction sentence formulating observational criteria of application for non-T_1:

$$\forall x[\alpha(x) \rightarrow \sim T_1(x)],$$

for, if T_1 refers to unobservable objects only, those to which it does *not* refer comprise clearly all observable ones. It is evident, however, that such negative criteria do not exhaust all meaning postulates for the theoretical terms in question. It surely does not suffice to say what objects are *not* electrons, when we are to specify the meaning of the term. Now it seems that for the terms in question certain positive criteria, though of a rather special nature, may be stated by means of postulates of the form (2.3). If the two-place predicate T_2, which occurs in all of them, is interpreted as the 'part-whole' relation, the postulates correspond to a very common type of statements about some theoretical objects, and may be regarded as meaning postulates for the given terms. A frequently quoted statement about electrons (highly oversimplified from a physical point of view) might serve as an example: 'If there appears a vapour trail in a cloud chamber x, then x contains (free) electrons'; or in a pedantic formulation:

'For every x: if there appears a vapour trail in a cloud chamber x, then there is an object y such that y is a part of x and y is a (free) electron'.

The postulate does not, of course, allow us to decide, on the basis of direct observation, whether an object is or is not an electron; it does allow us, however, to decide whether an object contains (free) electrons, and, in consequence, whether there exist any electrons, and so on.

A statement of form (2.3) represents a very weak type of meaning postulate. As the sole meaning postulate for T_1 and T_2, it is clearly non-creative, and determines the interpretations of T_1 and T_2 in a very slight degree only. But, as we have already mentioned, it never occurs, in scientific practice, as the single meaning postulate for both terms. Not only predicate T_2, but also T_1 are always governed by some other meaning postulates, which put additional restrictions on their interpretation.

Besides the simple type (2.3), there certainly occur, within actual empirical theories, some other, more complicated, types of meaning postulates with T–terms 'controlled' by an existential quantifier. We cannot, however, attempt their examination in this monograph.

Chapter Nine

MAIN TYPES OF STATEMENTS IN AN EMPIRICAL THEORY

One of the main problems in the logic of empirical theories concerns a distinction to be drawn between two kinds of components of any such theory: the '*a priori*' and the empirical ones. There arises with regard to any statement belonging to empirical theory a fundamental question: is its truth-value dependent on experience, or not? An account of the interpretation of an empirical theory T (or rather of its language L) as given in the preceding chapters makes it possible to distinguish between certain types of sentences of language L which differ just in the above mentioned respect. The main distinction here to be made is that between analytic, contradictory, and synthetic sentences of L.

I. ANALYTIC VERSUS SYNTHETIC SENTENCES OF L

The *analytic* sentences of language L, AN, may be identified, according to the usual procedure, with the logical consequences of the set MP of meaning postulates for T–terms of language L:

$$AN = Cn(MP).$$

Main Types of Statements in an Empirical Theory

It is easily seen that the truth of sentences AN is, in a sense, independent of experience. As, according to our assumption, set MP is always non-creative in the sense of condition (i), it is guaranteed in advance that family M^* defined with its help is a non-empty one and thus provides an interpretation for language L. Now, it can be shown that $AN \subseteq VER(M^*)$, and, consequently, that $AN \subseteq Ver$, on the basis of the definition of M^* alone (with the help, of course, of other syntactical and semantical definitions and theorems belonging to the metalanguage of L), and so independently of any empirical findings, in particular, of what the models of M_o^* might turn out to be. On the other hand, AN are clearly the only sentences of L whose truth can be established in such a way. If a sentence α is to be true in all models of M^* independently of whatever family of models M_o^* may happen to be, then α must be a logical consequence of MP. Otherwise, it would be false in some model of MP which might well prove a prolongation of a model from M_o^*, and thus a member of M^*. So, AN represents the set of all sentences in L whose truth is, in certain sense, independent of experience. Let us notice that

$$LV \subseteq AN,$$

though not conversely, for in all actual theories the set MP never consists of mere tautologies: it would then be simply superfluous. The negation of an analytic sentence of L will be called a *contradictory* one. The set of contradictory sentences of L, CN, will thus be defined as follows:

$$\alpha \in CN \leftrightarrow (\sim \alpha) \in AN.$$

In a similar way, as before, we have: $CN \subseteq FLS(M^*)$, and $CN \subseteq Fls$. It may then be maintained that the falsity of sentences CN is independent of experience. Notice that

$$LF \subseteq CN,$$

but not conversely: not all contradictory sentences of L must be logically false. Any sentence of L which is neither analytic nor contradictory will be included into the class SN of *synthetic* sentences of L:

$$SN = L - (AN \cup CN).$$

Now, with regard to any sentence of the class SN it certainly cannot be claimed that its truth-value is independent of experience: that it is true (or false) 'come what may'. But are we then entitled to say it has a truth-value that does depend on experience? In the case of certain kinds of synthetic sentences such an assumption does not seem to be justified. A distinction between determinate and indeterminate sentences of L proves to be decisive here.

II. DETERMINATE VERSUS INDETERMINATE SENTENCES OF L

The existence of these two kinds of sentences in L results from a fundamental feature of the interpretation of language L: its ambiguity. The interpretation of L given by family M^* is never unique. This is partly due to a similar character of the interpretation of its sublanguage L_o, given by family M_o^*, and partly due to the character of meaning postulates for language L itself. Owing to the notorious vagueness of all O–terms, family M_o^* contains always

more than one model of L_o. Now, since the meaning
postulates for T–terms fulfil the semantic condition
of non-creativity, family M^* will contain at least as
many models of L as family $M_o{}^*$. But, as a rule,
the meaning postulates do not determine the interpretation of T–terms (for a given interpretation of
O–terms) uniquely; so family M^* will, in fact, contain
more elements than family $M_o{}^*$. The interpretation
of L is, thus, 'doubly' ambiguous: to every model
from the numerous family $M_o{}^*$ there correspond a
number of models in family M^*. L, a language of an
empirical theory T, belongs, just as a purely observational language L_o, to the class of semantically
indeterminate languages. All that has been said about
this class of languages in previous chapters is thus true
of language L. In particular, there may be distinguished
in L three kinds of sentences mentioned before:

   (i) true in all models of M^*, $VER(M^*)$,
   (ii) false in all models of M^*, $FLS(M^*)$,
   (iii) true in some models of M^* and false in others.

The first two make up the class DT of *determinate*
sentences of L:

$$DT = VER(M^*) \cup FLS(M^*).$$

All the remaining sentences of L are *indeterminate*.
This is, undoubtedly, an important distinction. The
role played by indeterminate statements in actual
scientific inquiry seems highly problematic. It has
even been questioned, as we have mentioned before,
whether they possess any 'absolute' truth-value, i.e.
whether they might be said to be simply true or false,
and in what sense, if any. Be that as it may, they
certainly may be said to be undecidable statements.
One cannot validate or falsify a sentence which under

one intended interpretation turns out to be true and under another false. So, it seems rather doubtful whether an indeterminate sentence might qualify as a sentence whose truth-value depends on experience.

It is now clear what kind of sentences of language L do, in fact, belong to the class DT. Its definition may be expanded as follows:

$$\alpha \in DT \leftrightarrow$$

$$\leftrightarrow \forall \mathfrak{M}[\exists \mathfrak{M}_o \in M_o{}^*(\mathfrak{M}Prol\mathfrak{M}_o) \wedge MP \subseteq Ver(\mathfrak{M}) \rightarrow$$

$$\rightarrow \alpha \in Ver(\mathfrak{M})] \vee \forall \mathfrak{M}[\exists \mathfrak{M}_o \in M_o{}^*(\mathfrak{M}Prol\mathfrak{M}_o) \wedge$$

$$\wedge MP \subseteq Ver(\mathfrak{M}) \rightarrow \alpha \in Fls(\mathfrak{M})].$$

Now, it is easy to see that all analytic and contradictory sentences of L are included into DT:

$$AN \cup CN \subseteq DT.$$

All synthetic sentences of L which belong to language L_o will also be included into DT provided they belong to the class DT_o, i.e. to determinate observation sentences:

$$DT_o \subseteq DT.$$

And what about synthetic sentences of L which do not belong to L_o, i.e. which contain some of the T–predicates? We shall illustrate this case for a simple language L with a one-place theoretical predicate T_1 introduced by the following conditional definition as its only meaning postulate:

(1) $\qquad \forall x[O_1(x) \rightarrow (T_1(x) \leftrightarrow O_2(x))].$

Here, all sentences containing T_1 which by virtue of postulate (1) are translatable into a determinate observation sentence will clearly belong to DT. Take, e.g. sentence $\exists x(O_1(x) \wedge T_1(x))$. It is equivalent, on the basis of (1), to the following sentence of L_o: $\exists x(O_1(x) \wedge O_2(x))$; if the latter is included in DT_o, the former will belong to DT. But sentences of L which do not meet that requirement can, under certain conditions, also belong to the class of determinate sentences of L. The sentence $\exists x \, T_1(x)$, not translatable into any sentence of L_o by virtue of (1) alone, will belong to DT if, and only if, either $\exists x(O_1(x) \wedge O_2(x))$ or $\forall x(O_1(x) \wedge \sim O_2(x))$ is true in all models of $M_o{}^*$, i.e. belongs to $VER(M_o{}^*)$.

The last example exhibits a peculiar feature of the concept of determinateness as defined above. It shows that membership in the class DT may be a matter of experience. Whether a sentence, like $\exists x \, T_1(x)$, is or is not determinate clearly depends on experience, viz. on what the models of family $M_o{}^*$ are like. This is the reason why the set DT (or rather $SN \cap DT$) can hardly be identified with the set of *empirically meaningful* sentences of language L, in spite of the apparent plausibility of such a suggestion. It seems, in short, that the question of empirical meaningfulness, in contrast to the question of truth, should never be a matter of experience. In consequence, there arises a need for some concept of determinateness which will not be dependent on experience in the way in which the concept of DT is. It must then be a concept which does not refer to any particular family $M_o{}^*$. This may be done in at least two different ways. We arrive thus at two new concepts of a determinate sentence, DT_1 and DT_2, a stronger and a weaker one.

$$\alpha \in DT_1 \leftrightarrow \forall \mathfrak{M}_o \{ \forall \mathfrak{M} [\mathfrak{M} Prol \mathfrak{M}_o \wedge MP \subseteq Ver(\mathfrak{M}) \rightarrow$$
$$\rightarrow \alpha \in Ver(\mathfrak{M})] \vee \forall \mathfrak{M} [\mathfrak{M} Prol \mathfrak{M}_o \wedge$$
$$\wedge MP \subseteq Ver(\mathfrak{M}) \rightarrow \alpha \in Fls(\mathfrak{M})] \};$$

93

Main Types of Statements in an Empirical Theory

$$\alpha \in DT_2 \leftrightarrow \exists \mathfrak{M}_o \{ \forall \mathfrak{M} [\mathfrak{M} Pro l \mathfrak{M}_o \wedge MP \subseteq Ver(\mathfrak{M}) \rightarrow$$

$$\rightarrow \alpha \in Ver(\mathfrak{M})] \vee \forall \mathfrak{M} [\mathfrak{M} Pro l \mathfrak{M}_o \wedge$$

$$\wedge MP \subseteq Ver(\mathfrak{M}) \rightarrow \alpha \in Fls(\mathfrak{M})]\}.$$

Let us compare them briefly. We have of course: $DT_1 \subseteq DT_2$, and $DT \subseteq DT_2$ (as $M_o{}^*$ is never empty); it should be noticed, however, that $DT_1 \subseteq DT$ is not generally true. According to both concepts DT_1 and DT_2, all analytic and contradictory sentences of L will belong, as before, to determinate sentences of L:

$$AN \cup CN \subseteq DT_1, \ AN \cup CN \subseteq DT_2.$$

In contrast, however, to DT, both DT_1 and DT_2 will include all sentences of the sublanguage L_o:

$$L_o \subseteq DT_1, \text{ and } L_o \subseteq DT_2;$$

all observation statements become determinate sentences of L, in the meanings being now considered. And how are we to classify synthetic sentences of L which do not belong to L_o? There appears to be a considerable difference between DT_1 and DT_2 in this respect. Let us illustrate it in the simple case of language L described above. According to the definition of DT_1, a sentence of L containing predicate T_1 will belong to DT_1 if, and only if, it is translatable, by virtue of postulate (1), into a sentence of language L_o. Thus $\exists x(O_1(x) \wedge T_1(x))$ will have to be qualified as DT_1, and $\exists x\, T_1(x)$ as non–DT_1. According to the definition of DT_2, all sentences of L which contain the predicate T_1 introduced by (1), and thus all sentences of language L whatsoever, will belong to DT_2; so here, not only $\exists x(O_1(x) \wedge T_1(x))$, but also $\exists x\, T_1(x)$ are reckoned among determinate sentences.

It is evident from these observations that neither DT_1 nor DT_2 depend on experience in the way in which DT does. Whether a sentence of L does or does not belong to DT_1 (or DT_2) can be decided 'a priori', without any empirical investigation. The intuitive content of all these concepts might be rendered roughly as follows. α is DT, if, and only if, α is determinate under the intended interpretation of the observational language L_o (given by family $M_o{}^*$); α is DT_1, if, and only if, α is determinate whatever the interpretation of L_o (given by a single model, not a family of models!) may be; α is DT_2 if, and only if, there exists at least one interpretation of L_o under which α is determinate. The last concept seems to capture the idea of empirical meaningfulness fairly well. If α is a sentence of L determinate in the sense of DT_2, α may not, in fact, possess any definite truth-value; but it has got 'a chance' to acquire it: to be true in all models of M^* or false in all of them. This depends on what the models of $M_o{}^*$ turn out to be like. If, on the other hand, α is not DT_2, it does not even possess that chance. Whatever the models of $M_o{}^*$ prove to be, α will be devoid of any definite truth-value; it is irremediably indeterminate. It seems thus that the class of empirically meaningful sentences of language L, in at least one meaning of this undoubtedly ambiguous notion, might be identified with the class $SN \cap DT_2$. Our example of language L discussed above confirms this suggestion. A language whose only theoretical predicate has been defined conditionally by means of observational vocabulary can hardly contain, besides analytic and contradictory statements, any empirically meaningless sentences.

Chapter Ten

TOWARDS A MORE REALISTIC ACCOUNT

The theories we have considered thus far cannot be taken straightforwardly as representing actual empirical theories. They are far too simple to be identified with any such theory. They correspond rather to certain extreme cases of what might be called a basic empirical theory, cases which hardly could be found in actual scientific practice. In the present chapter we will try to give an account, very condensed and cursory indeed, of theories which come somewhat nearer to actual empirical ones, though which still cannot be identified with the most typical of them.

I. The language L of an empirical theory T discussed by us thus far may be thought of as a result of *one* extension of the observational language L_o: it has been constructed from the latter by introducing into it one series of theoretical terms by means of one set of postulates. Now there certainly are empirical theories whose language cannot be conceived in this way. It must be considered rather as a result of *several* successive extensions of the initial language L_o. In explaining this situation, we shall here deal with the simplest case involving two such extensions only. A generalization to n extensions will be quite obvious. Let the languages L_o and L be the same as before. L_o is an observational language with predicates $O_1, \ldots, O_l$, and L a theoretical one which has been constructed from L_o by introducing into it predicates $T_1, \ldots, T_m$ with the help of postulates P. Interpretations of L_o and L are conceived as before. The former is given by family $M_o{}^*$, the latter by family M^*, which has been defined with the help of meaning postulates MP 'isolated' from P in accordance with conditions (i) and (ii). Now we are extending language L to a richer theoretical language L_1 by introducing into it a new series of theoretical predicates $T_1{}^1, \ldots, T_r{}^1$ with the help of a new set of postulates P_1. The extralogical vocabulary of L_1 consists thus of predicates $O_1, \ldots, O_l, T_1, \ldots, T_m, T_1{}^1, \ldots, T_r{}^1$, and models of L_1, symbolized by $\mathfrak{M}_1$, are $l + m + r + 1$—tuples of the type:

$$\langle U, R_1, \ldots, R_l, \ S_1, \ldots, S_m, \ S_1{}^1, \ldots, S_r{}^1 \rangle.$$

Now the question arises how the intended interpretation of language L_1 is to be determined. Our answer to it will be based on two assumptions, which in the situation being considered sound quite convincing. We shall assume, namely, that the intended interpretation of L_1 (a) preserves the existing interpretation of all terms belonging to language L, i.e. all O– and T–predicates, as given by family M^*; (b) determines the interpretation of all terms being introduced, i.e. all T^1–predicates, in accordance with postulates P_1. So, any model of L_1 which is to belong to (providing the interpretation for L_1) family $M_1{}^*$ must meet these two conditions: it must be a prolongation of some model of family M^*, and, at the same time, it must be a model of the set of meaning postulates for T_1-predicates, MP_1, 'contained' in set P_1.

The task of isolating the set of meaning postulates MP_1 from the whole set of postulates P_1 may be accomplished along the lines followed previously with regard to language L. Set MP_1 must fulfil conditions strictly analogous to conditions (i) and (ii) laid down for set MP. There is only one important difference. It results from the fact that, in contrast to M_o^*, family M^* has been determined by certain verbal means: every model of M^* is to be a model of set MP. So we know here in advance that, whatever the models of M^* may turn out to be, all statements of set MP must certainly be true in them. Thus, in formulating the corresponding conditions (i) and (ii) for set MP_1, we need not refer to all models of language L, wherever in the original formulations we have referred to all models of language L_o. It is possible to restrict these conditions to those models of L only in which the set MP is true. The semantic condition of non-creativity for set MP_1 will then read as follows:

(i) $\forall \mathfrak{M}[MP \subseteq Ver(\mathfrak{M}) \rightarrow \exists \mathfrak{M}_1(\mathfrak{M}_1 Prol\mathfrak{M} \wedge MP_1 \subseteq$
$\subseteq Ver(\mathfrak{M}_1))]$.

It entails, as before, the corresponding syntactic condition:

$$L \cap Cn(MP_1) \subseteq Cn(MP),$$

but, again, is not equivalent to it. The condition (ii) will here assume a somewhat involved form, but its intuitive content seems quite clear and might be explained similarly as before. In its formulation given below, symbol $\mathfrak{M}_1|$ denotes the fragment of model $\mathfrak{M}_1$ corresponding to language L:

$$\mathfrak{M} = \mathfrak{M}_1| \leftrightarrow \mathfrak{M}_1 Prol\mathfrak{M}.$$

(ii) $\forall \mathfrak{M}_1 \{ MP \subseteq (Ver(\mathfrak{M}_1|) \land \exists \mathfrak{M}_1'(\mathfrak{M}_1'Prol\mathfrak{M}_1| \land$

$$\land P_1 \subseteq Ver(\mathfrak{M}_1')) \to [MP_1 \subseteq Ver(\mathfrak{M}_1) \leftrightarrow$$

$$\leftrightarrow P_1 \subseteq Ver(\mathfrak{M}_1)]\}.$$

It might be argued now (we shall not repeat the arguments adduced earlier) that any set MP_1 of sentences of L_1 which satisfies the above conditions may be regarded as the set of meaning postulates 'contained' in the set of postulates P_1, determined by a pragmatic decision.

A family M_1^* which is to provide the interpretation of L_1 can thus be defined as follows:

$$\mathfrak{M}_1 \in M_1^* \leftrightarrow \mathfrak{M}_1| \in M^* \land MP_1 \subseteq Ver(\mathfrak{M}_1).$$

The analytic sentences of language L_1 will clearly include all logical consequences of both sets of meaning postulates:

$$AN_1 = Cn(MP \cup MP_1).$$

Other types of sentences in L_1 might be defined accordingly. Let us illustrate some points of the above exposition by means of a simple schematic example. Let L contain one T–predicate introduced by an explicit definition:

$$\forall x(T_1(x) \leftrightarrow \sim O_1(x)),$$

and let it be extended to L_1 by introducing into it, in turn, one T^1–predicate with the help of the following partial definition:

$$\forall x[(T_1(x) \to T_1{}^1(x)) \land (O_1(x) \to \sim T_1{}^1(x))].$$

99

Now it is easy to see that the set containing the above partial definition as the only postulate for $T_1{}^1$ fulfils the semantic condition of non-creativity just defined (in spite of entailing some non-tautological sentences of L) and, consequently, may be taken as the set MP_1 of meaning postulates for language L_1. Situations like this seem to be typical for the actual practice of constructing an empirical theory. Such theory is seldom created 'from nothing'; it is usually built on the basis of some other theories. Hence, the procedure of constructing its language often starts, not from a purely observational language like L_o, but rather from a theoretical one, like L. When building, say, some chemical theory, we base it normally on a physical one. We introduce its specific chemical terms, not into a purely observational language, but into a theoretical one, which employs a number of specific physical terms. These terms have already been interpreted, and we want to respect that interpretation. We take them then in their established meanings and with their help determine the meaning of our chemical terms. The situation falls, thus, clearly under the schema outlined above.

II. That schema, however, has been criticized as being unrealistic. It has been questioned, namely, whether in actual scientific practice we ever start from a purely observational language, when constructing a theoretical one. Convincing arguments have been adduced to the effect that no scientific language contains a part that might be identified with our language L_o. Let us recall that L_o is an observational language in a rather strict meaning. All its extralogical terms, all O–predicates, are assumed to be interpreted in a non-verbal, ostensive, way. They are governed by no meaning postulates so that a direct observation may suffice for their application. But there are no such terms, it is argued, within actual empirical theories. Every term in science is governed by some meaning postulates. Whether or not it applies in a given case cannot be decided on the sole basis of direct observation. Now, we must admit that it is, in fact, difficult to find a clear case of a purely observational term employed by an actual scientific theory. All scientific terms appear to be theoretical in nature. We could do justice to this situation in the following way. We retain our obser-vational language L_o unchanged, with its O–terms interpreted in purely ostensive way. But now we shall not include them into the vocabulary of an empirical theory T. Its language will contain T–terms only. The role of O–terms will be played here by some 'elementary' or 'basic' T–terms. This basic language, L_B, may be identified, not with the observational part of language L, but rather with its theoretical part, that is, with L from which all O–terms have been deleted. The vocabulary of L_B consists thus of predicates $T_1, \ldots, T_m$, and models, $\mathfrak{M}_B$, of L_B are the corresponding fragments of models $\mathfrak{M}$ of L, i.e. $m + 1$–tuples of the type:

$$\langle U, S_1, \ldots, S_m \rangle.$$

The former interpretation of language L, given by family M^*, remains unchanged. It determines the interpretation of language L_B, given by family M_B^* defined as follows:

$$\mathfrak{M}_B \in M_B^* \leftrightarrow \exists \mathfrak{M} \in M^* (\mathfrak{M} \, Pro \, I \mathfrak{M}_B).$$

There appear now, in contrast to L_o, non-tautological analytic sentences of L_B—logical consequences of MP expressible in language L_B:

$$AN_B = L_B \cap Cn(MP).$$

The basic language L_B may then be extended to a theoretical language in the proper sense along the lines pursued in transition from L to L_1 as described above. On this conception, the observational language L_o, which remains outside any scientific discourse, might be treated as a part of a prescientific, everyday discourse, or, perhaps, only as a useful epistemological fiction, which helps us to account for the kind of interpretation characteristic of an empirical language.

Chapter Eleven

CONCLUDING REMARKS

The picture of empirical theory and its interpretation as outlined in the preceding chapters is admittedly unrealistic. It has been considerably oversimplified to bring out more easily some of its essential features. Certain of the simplifications have been removed in the last chapter. But certain others, and very important too, have remained: they cannot be removed without greatly complicating our exposition. And they prevent us, in consequence, from giving a fair account of the most typical and important empirical theories. One of those simplifications will now be indicated briefly. It amounts to a rather astonishing fact: the theories considered do not include any mathematics, do not employ any mathematical apparatus. By the latter we do not only mean a certain set of terms and a certain set of theorems characterized in a purely syntactical way. As no special restrictions have been placed on the set of theoretical terms and the set of axioms of our theory T, they might well include any mathematical terms and theorems that are needed. But these terms and theorems become mathematical in nature only when suitably interpreted; to be mathematical, they must be assigned their standard mathematical interpretation. The only terms in theory T which, according to our assumption, are given a fixed interpretation in advance are the logical ones. The first-order predicate calculus with identity endowed with its standard interpretation constitutes the only common basis on which the theories considered have been founded. No mathematical theory has been presupposed by them. And so, they are not equipped with mathematical tools needed in science. In consequence, the language of empirical theories under consideration does not contain any quantitative terms. No measureable properties are expressible in it, and thus no quantitative laws, no statistical hypotheses. Such language is certainly too poor to be identified with any language of typical scientific theory, for instance, a physical one. And it cannot be enriched to the desired extent without abandoning some of our simplifying assumptions. First of all, we should have to extend our universe of discourse beyond the set of physical objects. It must, in addition, include some mathematical entities, e.g. the set of all real numbers. This is a comparatively harmless modification which would not involve any essential changes in our exposition; and it has actually been realized to some extent in recent literature. (See [14].) But it does not appear to be sufficient in order to supply a theory with mathematical tools needed in science like physics. If the tools are to be powerful enough, the theory cannot remain an elementary one. It has to employ the general concept of set, relation, function, etc., and so, independently of the type of its formalization, it must, in fact, belong to non-elementary (or higher order) theories. And this would complicate our exposition considerably. This is why, in this monograph, we have had to restrict our attention to elementary theories only. But it must be admitted that in doing so we have deprived ourselves of the possibility of doing justice to the most important empirical theories.

In conclusion, there remains one point which should be clarified. It pertains to a feature which our approach to empirical theories shares with a broad class of investigations usually classified under the name of 'logical analysis' or 'logical reconstruction' of scientific theories. The feature may be said to consist of abstracting from any processes of change and development. Actual scientific theories are certainly not timeless entities. They constantly change with time. First of all, a set of theorems of a given theory changes as a whole. At any time it includes statements which did not belong to it earlier, and which will cease to be theorems later. But what is even more important, and less conspicuous and hence sometimes overlooked, are changes within a given set of theorems, i.e. changes concerning the logical status of different theorems. What was previously treated as a factual hypothesis becomes a meaning postulate; an analytic statement turns into a synthetic one, and so on. These changes characterize, not only different stages in development of a given theory, but also different contexts, or situations, in which the theory is employed. In consequence, what is treated as one theory in scientific practice, cannot be treated so in logical considerations; it must be identified with a certain family of theories in our sense, rather than with a single one. A theory as considered by the logician is a fairly definite set of statements. Its language, its set of theorems are explicitly defined. There is assumed a clear-cut division of all theorems into analytic and synthetic, determinate and indeterminate. Such a theory can be identified with a 'cross-section' of an actual scientific theory only. And so, if we want to investigate the latter in its entirety—and this is necessary if we are to account for logical problems of its development—we must deal with the whole series of its logical 'cross-sections'. The logical technique resembles here a biological one. Logical reconstruction of a scientific theory is like making 'slices' of a living organism. This certainly distorts our original object of inquiry. But only then can it be put under a logical microscope.

BIBLIOGRAPHICAL NOTE

The literature of the subject is too vast to be given here. The following list contains a small selection of works from those which, available in English, bear immediately on the main problems dealt with in the monograph, and have actually been made use of in presenting the subject. A few references mentioned in the text are restricted only to those works which do not yet belong to 'classic', or 'text-book', entries, and upon which some parts of the monograph have substantially been based.

[1] AJDUKIEWICZ, K. 'The Axiomatic Systems From the Methodological Point of View'. *Studia Logica*, 9(1960).

[2] BRAITHWAITE, R. B. *Scientific Explanation*. Cambridge, 1953.

[3] CARNAP, R. 'Testability and Meaning'. *Philosophy of Science*, 3(1936), 4(1937).

[4] CARNAP, R. *Foundations of Logic and Mathematics*. Chicago, 1939.

[5] CARNAP, R. 'Meaning Postulates'. *Philosophical Studies*, 3(1952).

[6] CARNAP, R. 'The Methodological Character of Theoretical Concepts'. *Minnesota Studies in the Philosophy of Science I*. Minnesota, 1956.

[7] CARNAP, R. 'On the Use of Hilbert's ∈-operator in Scientific Theories'. *Essays on the Foundations of Mathematics*. Jerusalem, 1961.

Bibliographical Note

[8] HEMPEL, C. G. *Fundamentals of Concept Formation in Empirical Science.* Chicago, 1952.

[9] HEMPEL, C. G. 'The Theoretician's Dilemma'. *Minnesota Studies in the Philosophy of Science II.* Minnesota, 1958.

[10] KEMENY, J. G. 'A New Approach to Semantics'. *Journal of Symbolic Logic,* 21(1956).

[11] KOKOSZYŃSKA, M. 'On Deduction'. *The Foundations of Statements and Decisions.* Warszawa, 1965.

[12] KOTARBIŃSKA, J. 'On Ostensive Definitions'. *Philosophy of Science,* 27(1960).

[13] MEHLBERG, H. *The Reach of Science.* Toronto, 1958.

[14] MONTAGUE, R. 'Deterministic Theories'. *Decisions, Values and Groups II.* Oxford, 1962.

[15] ROGERS, R. 'A Survey of Formal Semantics'. *Form and Strategy in Science.* Dordrecht, 1964.

[16] STOPES-ROE, H. V. 'Some Considerations Concerning "Interpretative Systems".' *Philosophy of Science,* 25(1958).

[17] SUSZKO, R. 'Formal Logic and the Evolution of Knowledge'. *Problems in the Philosophy of Science.* Amsterdam, 1968.

[18] WÓJCICKI, R. 'Semantical Criteria of Empirical Meaningfulness'. *Studia Logica,* 19(1966).